The Transformation Keys

The Transformation Keys

Unleash Your Best Self: A Practical Guide to Transforming Your Life

Simon Kent & Claire Chapman

Quantum Twenty One Publishing

For permission requests, contact the publisher at simon.kent@quantumtwentyone.com

Cover design: Simon Kent & Claire Chapman

Vintage key image: Merydolla via canva.com

ISBN: 978-1-7393945-2-3

eBook: 978-1-7393945-3-0

Published by: Quantum Twenty One Publishing (Quantum Twenty One Ltd)

DISCLAIMER

The book "The Transformation Keys" is intended to provide readers with insights, strategies, and personal perspectives on the topic of personal transformation. The authors of this book are not medical professionals, and the content within does not constitute medical advice, diagnosis, or treatment.

The information shared in this book is based on the authors' personal experiences, research, and opinions. It is not intended to replace professional medical, psychological, or therapeutic advice. Each individual's circumstances are unique, and what works for one person may not be suitable for another.

The authors do not make any claims, promises, or guarantees regarding the outcomes or results that readers may experience by following the suggestions, techniques, or approaches discussed in this book. Personal transformation is a multifaceted and individualised journey that can be influenced by various factors.

Readers are strongly advised to consult with qualified medical professionals, mental health experts, therapists, or other relevant professionals before implementing any of the ideas or practices mentioned in this book. Any decisions made based on the information in this book are the sole responsibility of the reader.

The authors and publishers disclaim any liability for any direct or indirect consequences, losses, or damages that may arise from the use of or reliance on the information provided in this book. This includes but is not limited to, physical, mental, emotional, or financial outcomes.

By reading "The Transformation Keys," you acknowledge that the authors are not medical professionals and that any choices you make based on the content of this book are made at your own risk. It is recommended to seek personalised guidance from appropriate professionals for your circumstances.

Please consult with qualified professionals before making any significant decisions related to your health, well-being, or personal transformation.

ACKNOWLEDGEMENTS

As the primary author, I extend my heartfelt gratitude to my co-author and the love of my life, Claire. Your unwavering belief in me and your remarkable gifts have inspired many transformation keys within this book and laid the foundation for my own transformation.

After I survived a stroke caused by a brain haemorrhage in September 2021, I saw you envision a future for us. Together, we embarked on a life-changing journey fuelled by love, navigating challenges hand in hand. Throughout this shared path, transformation remained at our core – as a family, a couple, and individuals. Claire, your presence means the world to me. While I compiled and created the transformation keys in this book, it's only fitting to acknowledge that we authored this title together.

As co-authors, we wholeheartedly send our deep love and gratitude to our children – Bryony, Charlotte, Eva, Will, and Logan. Your vibrant energy and wisdom fill us with joy, and as you journey through adolescence and into adulthood, you always and individually teach us invaluable lessons. You are our driving inspiration, exceeding your years in wisdom, and infusing our family with a vibrant spirit that propels us forward.

Recognising our families also means appreciating the pivotal roles of our parents. Claire's parents, Anita and Roger, radiate a deep kindness and compassion. Your generosity, especially in the early stages of my stroke recovery, laid the groundwork for my transformation. To my late mother and father, Lorna and Richard, Mum, my understanding of you runs profound, and I have cherished memories of conversations that bring warmth to my heart and Dad, I now grasp the lessons and wisdom you imparted in your lifetime. You both demonstrated the power of forgiveness which echoes in my thoughts daily. My love for you both remains forever unwavering.

During the initial six months of my stroke recovery, as these transformation keys took shape, Claire and I wish to extend our profound appreciation to the NHS healthcare professionals and volunteers who became part of our journey. Their kindness, compassion, and expertise were pivotal in aiding me to regain fundamental abilities, such as walking. Their dedicated care significantly impacted the outcome, making all the difference.

Claire and I are equally thankful to remarkable individuals who selflessly invested time to proofread and offer invaluable feedback on the book's first draft. We extend our appreciation to Jason Gardiner, Anita Gough, Lee Gough, and Gemma Tullett – your insights will have notably enhanced the book's impact on its readers.

Furthermore, we want to convey our heartfelt gratitude to Sue Stone. Your exceptional guidance throughout the book's creation and publication, your eloquent foreword, and your role as the catalyst for Claire's own spiritual awakening journey hold immeasurable value. Your wisdom is boundless, and we hold deep appreciation for all that you are.

Lastly, each day, we express gratitude to the divine consciousness flowing through all existence, bestowing profound wisdom that guides us in every moment and grants us the transformation keys within this book.

Gemma and Kevin.
This is for you both. For your friendship and your unwavering love
and kindness.

The Transformation Keys is a testament to the incredible power of the human spirit and the potential for transformation in all of our lives. The authors, Simon Kent and his fiancé Claire Chapman, have faced immense adversity covering all aspects of life and come out of the other side with a new perspective that is truly inspiring.

Simon's hugely challenging experience for them both was one of resilience and determination. After suffering a near-death stroke, he was faced with the daunting task of rebuilding his life from scratch. He had to learn how to walk, talk and think again. But as Simon began the long road to recovery, with Claire's love, support and deep knowing they realised that Simon's stroke had given him a Gift: the opportunity to transform his life in ways he had never before imagined.

With Claire's encouragement and wisdom, what Simon discovered on this journey is that transformation requires a willingness to look inward, to confront our fears and shortcomings and to make difficult choices that challenge us to grow. The Transformation Keys is a guide to this process, a roadmap for anyone who is seeking to make meaningful changes in their life.

This practical guide is a powerful tool for anyone at any stage of their life. Whether you are facing a major life change, struggling with a personal challenge or simply seeking to live a more fulfilling life, this book offers pragmatic advice and inspiration that can help you along your journey. It will empower you to be open to change, to embrace uncertainty and to trust in yourself and the universe.

You will learn about the importance of self-care, the power of gratitude and the value of living a life of purpose. You will also discover many tools and exercises that can help you transform your own life.

In closing, I would like to say that The Transformation Keys is a remarkable book that has the power to transform lives. It is a testament to the resilience of the human spirit and the potential for transformation in all of us. I trust that you will find in its pages the inspiration and guidance to unlock your own transformational journey.

Well done Simon and Claire, a valuable practical guide to personal transformation for all!

Sue Stone
Author, Inspirational Speaker and Transformational Leader

HOW TO USE THIS BOOK

Thank you for choosing to purchase this practical guide of transformation keys. Within its pages, you will find a valuable reference filled with profound wisdom and practical steps to facilitate your transformation and enhance your overall well-being. Our intention is for these keys and accompanying actions to serve as a compass, enabling you to navigate your transformative journey with ease and kindness for yourself.

Embarking on a journey of personal transformation is seldom easy, and it's not uncommon for us to abandon the goals and visions we set for ourselves. We yearn for a life filled with joy, fulfilment, and purpose, yet often it remains elusive, shrouded in mystery. Hence, our intention, backed by unwavering confidence, is that this book will serve as a guiding light, empowering you to persevere on the path of your transformation. It may even ignite within you the inspiration to change a particular aspect of your life, unlocking the doors to a brighter future; unleashing your best self.

As the phrase suggests, personal transformation is inherently individual. It is a deeply personal journey that varies for each of us. What motivates and propels you forward may differ from what inspires someone else, and that's perfectly alright. There is no judgment or expectation for you to conform to a specific mould or attain a predetermined outcome in your transformation. Your journey of transformation is uniquely yours, shaped by your desires, values, and aspirations. Embrace the freedom to chart your path and remember that your transformation is solely yours to embrace and celebrate.

While compiling these transformation keys into this book, we had a vision of how it could be utilised. However, much like personal transformation itself, the way you choose to use this book is entirely within your control. Consider our suggestions as a helpful guide, but feel free to adapt and tailor the book to your own unique needs and preferences. Ultimately, the power lies in your hands to determine how this book will serve you best on your journey of personal transformation.

The book commences with a brief introduction, shedding light on the origin of the transformation keys and the circumstances that led to their discovery. As that particular story unfolded, it became clear that those very circumstances were instrumental in triggering Simon's own profound personal transformation. Following this introduction, each chapter of the book is dedicated to the transformation keys themselves.

Within the book, you will find a total of 124 transformation keys thoughtfully arranged with a short chapter for each key. Each transformation key chapter is structured uniformly to ease navigation through the book. Firstly, you will encounter the transformation key itself, followed by a descriptive interpretation describing the essence of the key in greater detail. Following the key and its descriptive text, you will find an action step or journal prompt, providing you with a practical way to apply the key to your own life. This intentional layout allows for a seamless flow of knowledge and hands-on application as you progress through the transformative journey within the book.

Feel free to explore the transformation keys at your own pace, whether you prefer browsing through them sequentially, or you might choose to pick keys randomly by selecting them in moments of quiet mindfulness.

The former sequential method flows with the natural highs and lows of Simon's own personal transformation during his recovery from haemorrhagic stroke. The full story of that recovery and transformation is documented in the book "The Gift". This sequential method is reflective of many personal transformation journeys with the ups and downs, the challenges and the moments of euphoria. It is a journey of profound transformation and in that sense, it is a blueprint that offers guidance to anyone embarking on any type of personal transformation.

On the other hand, the latter method is analogous to using this book somewhat like you might use oracle cards, where you could set an intention before "pulling" a card (or in this case, turning to a transformation key). This method makes this book a very supportive companion for those already progressing with any form of personal transformation journey.

If you choose the latter "oracle card" type of method, find a tranquil space, gently close your eyes, take a deep breath, and silently say in your mind,

> " At this moment, what do I need to know to support my transformation? "

Then, while keeping your eyes closed and allowing all other thoughts to dissipate, simply open the book to any page within The Transformation Keys section (chapters 1 -124). Let your intuition guide you to the exact key (chapter) that holds a message meant for you at that particular moment. Trust the serendipity of this process and embrace the wisdom that awaits you within the key that is presented.

Open your eyes and observe the transformation key that has been revealed to you. Take in the words and allow their meaning to resonate within you. This key has chosen you at this moment, offering guidance and insight on your journey of transformation. Embrace the message it holds and consider how it may apply to your life, empowering you to unlock new possibilities and embrace your path of growth.

In a tranquil and intentional manner, softly read the transformation key along with its description. Allow the words to sink in, engaging with their profound meaning. Afterwards, take a moment to pause and enter a state of meditation. Reflect upon the wisdom encapsulated within the key, allowing it to permeate your thoughts and feelings. Embrace this serene pause, cultivating a deeper understanding of how the key resonates with your journey of transformation.

When meditating on a transformation key, there are various approaches you can take. You may choose to deepen your breath, allowing each inhale and exhale to guide you into a state of calm. Alternatively, you can enhance the ambience by listening to soothing music that resonates with your soul. Another option is to simply revisit the transformation key, immersing yourself in its profound message. Feel free to explore a combination of these approaches or follow what feels right for you. Remember, there is no right or wrong method. As the saying goes, "You do you." The key (no pun intended) is to create a quiet space for this experience, free from any external distractions, so you can fully immerse yourself in the transformative process.

As you explore the transformation keys, you will see an associated action step or journal prompt. In our human experience, tangible transformation in the physical realm often requires taking some form of action. Consider making a personal commitment to wholeheartedly engage in the suggested action step or journal prompt, approaching it with self-love and kindness. Embrace the opportunity to immerse yourself in this transformative process. Notice how your "being"ness, your state of being, begins to shift and evolve as you integrate these actions and journal prompts into your life. Allow yourself to be open to the changes that unfold, fostering a deeper connection with your authentic self and embracing the transformative power within you.

As you delve into the transformation keys, you might encounter what seems like contradictions between some of them. For instance, the key of Vision might appear to contradict the key of Journey. However, it's essential to understand that all of these keys hold significance on the path of personal transformation.

Let's explore this apparent contradiction further.

While it may seem counterintuitive to simultaneously focus on a vision while embracing the journey, the secret lies in achieving both. You can hold a clear vision for your desired outcome while fully immersing yourself in the present journey. It's about striking a harmonious balance between the two.

In closing this section, as you continue on your path of transformation, it's crucial to maintain a deliberate focus on your vision, approaching it with intention, determination and a calm sense of knowing. Keep your ultimate goal in clear sight, anchoring yourself in the purpose that propels your journey. Simultaneously, cherish and fully appreciate the transformative process itself - the moments of triumph, the challenges overcome, and the invaluable lessons learned. Recognise the growth embedded in each experience along the way, embracing the journey as an indispensable aspect of your transformation. Find joy and fulfilment in the small victories, and let the process shape you as you progress toward manifesting your envisioned future.

We would be honoured if you consider us your companions

on this journey of change. These keys are here to offer support, with the understanding that love and compassion are important. Let them guide you, cheering you on and standing by your side. Allow these keys to nurture you with self-love and compassion, giving you strength wherever you are in life. Think of them as tools for growth and empowerment as you navigate your unique transformation journey.

INTRODUCTION

To transform is to change, and change is an inevitable and continuous part of life. We are constantly changing - our physical bodies, our careers, our relationships, and even our minds and beliefs about situations. Change is pervasive and ever-present.

Moreover, we are in a constant state of change. If you ever watch film or video footage of cell reproduction within the body, you'll soon realise that change is happening all the time. Additionally, we are hurtling through the physical universe at over one million miles per hour, so it's not surprising that change is constant and perpetual.

If you're someone who thinks you don't like change, well, we're afraid to say that despite your adversity to it, change is unavoidable and already happening. So, put on your seat belt because this journey called life is one heck of a ride!

It is commonly believed that change occurs outside of our control, positioning us as passive recipients of its effects. This victimised approach to change is disempowering. The truth is, that we are far more powerful than mere victims of change.

Each one of us can actively influence change in our lives to align with our preferences. We create our version of reality, and it all starts with our thoughts and feelings. When we change our perspective on the world, our reality transforms. It is not uncommon to encounter individuals who repeatedly replay negative scenarios and events from their past and then complain that things never change or work out for them. Do you know why? It's simple - they are recreating the same scenarios and reality repeatedly. They are not changing how they view themselves and the world around them.

Some might say this doesn't make sense, so let's consider this example. If someone experienced a difficult situation in the past, it likely triggered an emotional reaction. Among the various outcomes, this emotional experience may have caused energy and memory to become trapped in their body. To further illustrate this, imagine a scenario where a teacher reprimanded a child in class for asking a question that the teacher deemed silly or inappropriate. The teacher's scolding elicited a range of emotional responses at the time, such as embarrassment and sadness. These emotional responses could also manifest in physical reactions. For instance, the child, being young, might have started crying or even lost control of their bladder, resulting in further embarrassment and anguish, or in other words, additional forms of pain. If that wasn't enough, the knock-on effect is even greater. As humans, what we unconsciously do in moments such as these, is add meaning to the event. In other words, we make it *mean* something about ourselves. For example, this child could now add meanings such as "I am silly", "I am wrong", "I should never speak out" or any other negative meaning that they create in the mind and believe it to be *real*. When we do this, the interplay between emotions and meanings continues to live with us throughout our lives, unless we actively address them and choose to change.

Now, let's fast forward our example to adult life. Imagine the same person has an opportunity to present to a team of work colleagues, speak in front of an audience at a conference, or record a video blog on social media. Let's also consider that this presentation or video blog could potentially propel them towards a career goal or life aspiration. In other words, the scenario carries with it a high degree of emotional attachment. Having scenarios with a high degree of emotional attachment is not at all uncommon for a great many people.

Going into this situation, the individual, who still holds hidden beliefs that they are "silly", "wrong" or "should never speak out", is triggered, resulting in the same emotional response from the above childhood trauma. Based on this cocktail of emotions and meanings, the individual might retreat from, what could have been a transformative and fulfilling experience, to avoid any potential pain. In other words, they go into a limiting *protective* state, shielding themselves from pain.

As illogical as this may sound to the rational mind, such situations can often occur for many people. The fear of pain can significantly hinder personal growth and hold individuals back in various aspects of life.

This is a prime example of what we mean by repeatedly recreating one's reality. The presence of hidden emotions and meanings, along with trapped energy, generates forms of fear, which in turn, leads to the avoidance of pain and associated thoughts. These avoidance behaviours, driven by unconscious memories, become significant obstacles that prevent many people from progressing in their lives and creating the change they desire. As a result, their reality remains unchanged, resembling what it was before. In the previous example, the avoidance of pain would manifest as fear of "embarrassment", "judgment" and "being seen".

In terms of our life experience, we often find ourselves effectively standing still, feeling "stuck" without any transformation towards our goals and aspirations. This irony becomes apparent when we consider that almost every aspect of the physical body has undergone countless changes since any original trauma. Yet, the trapped emotion and memory within us can create a reaction as if nothing has changed at all. This stagnation can be profoundly debilitating in terms of fear, and our ability to fully express ourselves and experience the richness of life. Regrettably, many people find themselves caught in this type of scenario, leading to a less fulfilling existence than what is truly possible. The unfortunate truth is that they are not living up to their truest expression or potential, resulting in a sense of unhappiness and unfulfillment. Personal transformation offers an escape from such an unfulfilled life.

As mentioned earlier, our thoughts and feelings have the

power to shape our reality. Thoughts can evoke feelings, and in turn, feelings can influence our thoughts. When these thoughts and feelings take on a negative nature life may seem to consistently fall short of our desires.

The good news is that you have the power to shape your future reality. If you desire a change or transformation in your life, you hold the power to make it happen right now, in this very moment.

You might be asking, what makes you both, Simon and Claire, qualified to write this book?

That's a valid question. What qualifies us to write this? Who are we to claim such authority? The deeper truth is that we are just as qualified as you, and you are just as qualified as either of us. This knowledge already resides deep within your soul, but it may have been forgotten over time. So, in essence, we are not presenting you with something entirely new; instead, we are simply reminding you of what you have momentarily forgotten.

For me, Simon, I had an experience that reminded me of this knowledge in a very serious way and it was a matter of life or death.

On September 11, 2021, my life took a sudden turn when I experienced a hemorrhagic stroke in the cerebellum region of my brain. This type of stroke, also known as a brain haemorrhage or medically referred to as a Posterior ICH, occurs when blood vessels within the brain rupture, causing bleeding. For those unfamiliar with this condition, it involves a bleed within the brain itself. In my case, the stroke was a result of the stress I had experienced throughout my adult life, which led to elevated blood pressure. It's important to note that such strokes often result in fatality, but fortunately, I survived.

Leading up to that moment, I maintained a fit lifestyle with a healthy diet. I abstained from smoking and excessive alcohol consumption. Together with Claire, we led a fulfilling life, raising our blended family of five children. Everything seemed to be going well, until suddenly, like a lightning strike, our world was completely upended in an unexpected and split-second moment. The impact was profound, not only for me but also for Claire and our entire family. On reflection, although I thought my life was all great before the stroke, I was often anxious and I was almost certainly stressed.

At the age of 53, surviving the stroke was nothing short of a miracle. Circumstances prevented me from reaching a hospital for 13 hours, and I received no immediate medical intervention, except for a CT scan to confirm the brain haemorrhage. Instead, I found myself in the embrace of divine consciousness, which some might refer to as God. Here, I don't use the term "God" in a religious sense, but rather to denote the universal life force or divine life-consciousness that energises the entire universe, including all living beings. It was this force that sustained me through those critical moments.

The experience of the haemorrhage was a profound spiritual

awakening that surpassed any expectations I had. Despite the challenges, I not only survived but continue to navigate the ongoing process of recovery and transformation, which may extend throughout my lifetime. For two weeks, I was hospitalised and faced the daunting task of relearning everything from scratch. Basic functions such as walking, self-care, and personal hygiene had to be rediscovered. This journey of personal transformation was intense, encompassing various aspects of my being: physical, emotional, spiritual, mental, intellectual, and even financial. I essentially rebuilt and transformed my entire existence, as my brain had suffered severe injury and damage. The cause of my transformation was not of my choosing, but having faced a very bleak future, that appeared to me at the time, to be "out of the blue", I then had to make a choice. Would I yield to the effects of the stroke or would I choose a different path? A path of recovery and personal transformation.

During the initial few weeks of my recovery, I distinctly recall Claire expressing the belief that the stroke would ultimately be a gift; an opportunity for a fresh start. It's worth noting that Claire possessed a deeper spiritual connection than I did at the time. While I was in no physical or mental condition to debate her perspective, my human-ego mind couldn't help but question, "Yeah, sure thing Claire. What on earth are you talking about? How could this situation possibly be considered a gift?" In those early days, my shattered mind wasn't prepared to accept that such an awful situation could be considered a gift; it was beyond my capabilities at that time and yet my inner being listened to Claire with a knowing that she would indeed be right.

It has been over two years since that fateful day, and while many perceive me as recovered, my transformation continues. I have evolved from being a patient confined to a hospital bed to a man who now enjoys newfound activities such as walking rugby, sailing, writing and publishing, and an unexpectedly profound spiritual connection, who would have known? Each day, I stroll through fields and woodlands with our faithful canine companion, sometimes alone but often with Claire. Also, each day, I spend intentional time writing my thoughts and internal conversations with the Source of All, whom I address as "God". I commemorated the stroke's first anniversary by joyously participating in a dance festival in London. I relish precious moments with my family and our life together. I teach, coach, and engage in short-term contract work in the realm of Business IT and have a passion for continuous learning. With aspirations for the future, I can confidently say that life is good - albeit different, but undeniably good. To become the new version of myself, I underwent a comprehensive personal transformation across all facets of my being.

During the first six months of stroke recovery and transformation, I embarked on a blogging journey on social media, documenting my experiences. Little did I anticipate that this humble blog would serve as the foundation for a profoundly personal and cathartic book, aptly titled "The Gift." As I poured my heart and soul into the pages of "The Gift", "The

Transformation Keys" took shape, each key representing a pivotal moment in my recovery and transformation. As readers delve into the contents of "The Gift", they will discover the precise origins of these transformation keys and witness the profound impact they had on my journey. With great certainty, I affirm Claire's foresight - the gift bestowed by the stroke gradually unveiled itself in diverse and remarkable ways, with the transformation keys shining brightest among them.

As the transformation keys took shape within the pages of "The Gift", a profound realisation dawned upon me - an entirely new book was in the making, seemingly effortlessly. And now, dear reader, you possess that very book - "The Transformation Keys." As I crafted the words of this book, it became strikingly apparent that its impact transcended personal catharsis. Instead, it blossomed into a self-help guide with universal appeal, capable of empowering individuals worldwide, irrespective of individual circumstances. It is with utmost conviction that I affirm your inevitable success, as you embark on this enlightening journey. Within these pages, you will find the tools and wisdom to unlock your transformation, enabling you to embrace your true potential and create a life of profound fulfilment. May this book bring you immense value and guide you towards the extraordinary success that awaits you.

One of the most profound revelations that emerged from my experience with the brain haemorrhage was the crystal-clear understanding that every one of us holds the power to shape our unique version of reality. It became strikingly evident that what we commonly perceive as "reality" is, in fact, a creation of the intricate workings of our brains.

In an instant, when a 4cm surge of blood inundated my cerebellum, it unleashed irreparable havoc on essential neurons, synapses, neural transmitters, and neural pathways, leading to an immediate and profound change in my perception of reality. The damage inflicted upon that intricate neural network was so severe that the once familiar horizontal plane of what we call reality transmuted into a perpendicular orientation, and vice versa. My physical worldview, firmly anchored in the horizontal, was abruptly upended by a jarring 90-degree shift. It was a nightmarish ordeal.

Surviving such a traumatic brain injury is an outcome that, sadly, eludes many individuals. It was an experience I have no desire to relive, as I'm sure you can imagine. Fortunately, the harrowing distortion of my reality ceased after a distressing night, thanks to a bona fide miracle, physiotherapy and years dedicated to my recuperation. Now, for the most part, I have regained full functionality, except for the occasional stumble as I navigate my restored reality, which thankfully aligns with the expected horizontal and vertical planes.

While crafting "The Gift" and witnessing the emergence of these transformation keys, I came to a further realisation. Though the narrative stemmed from my journey and the keys found their origin in my writing, I couldn't ignore the fact that many of the underlying themes and thoughts behind these keys were originally bestowed upon me by Claire. Her profound wisdom runs deep and holds the power to transform truly. I dare say that my recovery and personal transformation would not have reached the level it has without Claire's invaluable presence and guidance.

Now, let's hear from Claire.

For me, Claire, transformation runs through my very core. I am an individual whose life took an unexpected turn in 2013 and it was in that pivotal moment that I faced a profound breakdown that shattered the facade of the life I thought I knew. Fuelled by a fearless spirit, and hearing a clear message from my soul saying "You have to help yourself", I delved headfirst into the world of personal development and self-discovery. These words were my awakening moment to divine consciousness, which I too refer to as "God" or "Source Energy". My background in engineering along with business and finance served as a foundation, but it was the experience of my spiritual awakening and profound transformation that truly shaped my understanding of the human journey.

It's not about the titles or degrees; it's about the raw, unfiltered experience of rebuilding oneself. Through the trials of my metamorphosis, I unearthed a passion for guiding others on their transformative paths. This passion led to the creation of my self-development business, where I dedicate myself to helping individuals redefine their relationships with themselves, money, and abundance.

When Simon faced his own darkest hour, I instantly felt a positive "knowing" deep within me, that *only* good would come from this event. I heard an almost silent whisper that I knew, despite the obvious anguish, that the stroke would become the making of him; it would be his truly transformative "gift."

> This is an opportunity for him to relive his life differently.

Of course, it is very rare to form the conclusion that the situation with Simon would turn out to be a gift. But when I felt and heard that guidance from deep within my soul, it became the beacon by which both Simon and I would tap into source energy. I do not doubt that deliberately accessing source energy ultimately propelled his remarkable recovery and transformation, and my own deeper resilience and strength. In other words, it was an opportunity for further transformation for us both.

Hence, it seems that we are indeed qualified to delve into the realm of personal transformation.

While some may perceive these as mere projections stemming from our personal experiences, our intention is far from projection. Instead, it is rooted in love and compassion, as we wholeheartedly share these transformation keys with you.

As we conclude this section and you journey onward through these pages, our wish is for you to discover inspiration and guidance. May you also summon the courage to embrace your transformative journey as these keys resonate with you in a deeply personal way.

In closing, as highlighted earlier, change is an ever-present facet of life. Yet, intentional change sets itself apart from unconscious shifts. Deliberate and conscious change is a choice, a seemingly straightforward distinction that imparts immense power to personal transformation. Here's to embarking on your intentional and consciously chosen path of personal transformation!

With love,

Simon & Claire

CONTENTS

The Transformation Keys

CONTENTS

CONTENTS

CONTENTS

CONTENTS

CONTENTS

CONTENTS

CONTENTS

CONTENTS

The Transformation Keys

Kindness

> *Transformation takes determination. Find grace*
> *for yourself as you face hardships. Forgive yourself*
> *and others when you feel in a low vibrational energy*
> *(mood). You're lucky to be alive. Love yourself. You*
> *are worthy.*

Transformation is not an easy process and it takes a lot of determination to push through the hardships and challenges that come with it.

It's important to remember that we are all human and we all face challenges of varying degrees of difficulty. It's important to be kind to ourselves as we face these challenges and to forgive ourselves and others when we are feeling down.

It's also important to remind ourselves to be grateful for every moment of life. It can be easy to get caught up in negative thoughts and feelings but it's essential to shift our focus to the positive and to love ourselves for who we are.

Remember that we are worthy and that we deserve to live the life we want. We can overcome obstacles and challenges with determination, grace, and self-love. We can create the life we desire, but it's important to remember that it's a journey, and it takes time and patience.

> **Action Step**: Take a few moments each day to practice self-kindness, gratitude, and forgiveness, allowing yourself to acknowledge and accept the challenges you face while cultivating a positive mindset and embracing your worthiness for personal growth and transformation.

Progress

Chart your progress; You will be amazed at your transformation.

Transformation is a powerful force that can occur in various ways and time frames. For those who have experienced a significant health event, like a stroke, transformation can be a lengthy process of recovery and rehabilitation.

However, the concept of time is subjective and influenced by our perception of reality. Regardless of the duration, tracking the progress of transformation is a powerful ally.

Charting your journey provides feedback and evidence, creating momentum and positive energy. It allows you to see how far you have come, and to celebrate every win along the way, whether they are small wins or big wins.

For example, stabilising blood pressure after my stroke was, and still is, a crucial set of milestones in recovery. Tracking my blood pressure readings and making medication adjustments helped to determine which combination of drugs was/is most effective for my body.

Another powerful tool for tracking progress is keeping a daily journal.

Journaling helps to reflect on the transformation journey and identify areas of growth, improvement, and gratitude. Whether it's using a timeline, a daily journal, or another approach, the act of charting your progress can be motivating and inspiring.

> **Journal Prompt:** Reflect on your transformation journey, whether related to health or personal growth, and explore the ways in which tracking and charting your progress, whether through journaling or other methods, has provided you with valuable insights, motivation, and a sense of accomplishment along the way.

3

Breathe

The power of breath will amaze you.

The power of breath is truly amazing, and it has the ability to transform our physical, emotional and mental well-being.

Breathing exercises, such as pranayama, can help to reduce stress and anxiety, lower blood pressure, and improve sleep. It can also help to improve focus and concentration, which can be beneficial for all aspects of our lives.

Breathing deeply and mindfully can also have a positive impact on our emotional well-being. When we feel stressed or anxious, our breath tends to become shallow, which can make us feel more tense. By taking slow, deep breaths, we can activate the parasympathetic nervous system, which helps to calm the body and mind.

In addition, certain breathing techniques such as meditation, yoga and mindfulness practice can help to bring more awareness and clarity to our thoughts and emotions, encouraging a more peaceful and balanced state.

By incorporating breathing exercises into our daily routine, we can improve our overall health and well-being, and bring more awareness and balance to our thoughts and emotions. Breath is a powerful tool that we can use to improve our lives and it will amaze you with the positive impact it can have on your body and mind.

Action Prompt: Take a few moments each day to engage in a breathing exercise of your choice, such as deep belly breathing or guided pranayama practice, allowing the transformative power of your breath to reduce stress, improve focus, and promote emotional well-being.

4

Acceptance

> *You're alive; Learn to surrender and accept what is; You can find peace where you are right now; You are on a journey*

Being alive is a gift and it is important to learn to surrender and accept what is.

It can be difficult to accept difficult situations and circumstances, but when we can learn to let go of our resistance and accept what is, we open ourselves up to finding peace in the present moment.

It is important to remember that we are all on a journey, and that journey is unique to each and every one of us. We may encounter obstacles and challenges, but it is through these experiences that we learn and grow.

Instead of focusing on what we cannot change, we can focus on what we can control – our thoughts, attitudes and actions.

Finding peace where you are right now is possible. It starts with a shift in perspective and a willingness to let go of our attachment to certain outcomes. We can learn to find peace in the present moment by practicing mindfulness, meditation, or other forms of self-care.

Journal Prompt: Explore life as a gift and the significance of accepting the present. Acknowledge challenges as opportunities for growth. Shift focus to control thoughts and actions, fostering peace. Practice mindfulness and self-care for present-moment serenity.

5

Imagination

Your imagination is so powerful; Put it to work and imagine the beautiful future that you can create; This current reality will pass.

Our imagination is incredibly powerful, and it is a tool that we can use to create a beautiful future for ourselves.

The ability to imagine and envision a future that we want is the first step in making it a reality. We can use our imagination to visualise the life we want, the people we want to surround ourselves with, and the experiences we want to have.

One of the most important things to remember is that this current reality will pass. Life is constantly changing and evolving, and what may seem like a difficult or impossible situation now, will change in the future if we can hold the vision in our imagination.

Instead of getting caught up in the fear and worry associated with a current challenge, we can use our imagination to envision a future that we want and take steps towards making it a reality.

We can use our imagination to come up with creative solutions, think outside the box, and find new ways of approaching obstacles. When we put our imagination to work, we open ourselves up to new possibilities and opportunities.

Action Step: Take dedicated time each day to journal and engage in the creative exercise of visualising your desired future outcome, allowing yourself to explore the emotions, actions, and specific steps needed to manifest that vision into reality.

6

Learning

> *FAIL means First Act In Learning; It's great to fail,*
> *it means you are learning.*

I first heard about this FAIL anagram at a seminar in Toronto, Canada with the late Bob Proctor. I don't know who came up with the original concept, but it's a brilliant way to look at failure.

We've been taught throughout our lives that failure is bad, but I disagree. When you adopt the First Act In Learning mindset, it can change your entire approach to life.

We are constantly subject to change, and when we want to intentionally or consciously implement change or transformation in our lives, we must be prepared for some parts that may not work quite as intended.

Think about a scientific experiment to prove or disprove an idea or theory. It's undertaken with the intention to learn from the outcome. This is the same approach. When things don't go quite as planned or as originally imagined, what can you learn? What can you take forward into the next step of the creation process as you create your transformation?

When we see failure as a learning opportunity, we open ourselves up to new possibilities and growth. It allows us to approach challenges and obstacles with a different perspective and to see the bigger picture.

Instead of getting caught up in the negative emotions associated with failure, we can focus on the valuable lessons and insights that come with it.

Journal Prompt: Reflect on a recent experience of failure or setback, and explore the valuable lessons and insights you gained from it, considering how embracing the "First Act In Learning" mindset can shift your perspective on failure and empower you to approach future challenges with a growth-oriented mindset.

7

Judgement

Drop all judgement; Don't judge others and most of all, don't judge yourself

Judgement is a natural human tendency, but it can often be harmful to ourselves and others.

When we judge others, we create a barrier between us and them, making it difficult to understand and connect with them.

When we judge ourselves, we can become trapped in negative thoughts and self-doubt, which can lead to feelings of low self-worth and self-esteem.

One of the most important things we can do to improve our relationships with others and ourselves is to drop all judgment.

This means letting go of our preconceptions and assumptions about others and approaching them with an open mind and heart.

It also means being kind and compassionate towards ourselves, and not judging ourselves harshly for our mistakes or shortcomings.

When we drop all judgement, we are able to see others and ourselves more clearly, and to connect with them on a deeper level. We become more understanding, empathetic and compassionate, which can lead to more meaningful and fulfilling relationships.

Action Step: Practice cultivating non-judgmental awareness by consciously pausing before making judgements about others or yourself, and instead, approach situations with an open mind and heart, fostering understanding, empathy, and compassion in your interactions and self-reflection.

8

Miracle

Love your brain; Love yourself; You are amazing

Our brains are truly a marvel of nature, capable of coordinating and sequencing the complex neurological signalling that occurs constantly.

However, it wasn't until I experienced a traumatic brain injury from a brain haemorrhage that I truly realised the complexity and miracle of the human brain.

Through my experience, I came to understand that our brains are nothing short of a miracle and that by extension, we too are a miracle.

Our brain is the source of our power, intelligence, and ability to function. It enables us to do seemingly simple tasks, like tying shoe laces without looking, with ease and without conscious thought. However, this task is actually a complex coordination of various bodily functions and neurology, all controlled by the brain, typically whilst also having a conversation or myriad other distractions, and meanwhile, all our essential bodily functions and organs are working in the background.

This transformation key has been a powerful reminder for me of the incredible capabilities of the human brain and the infinite potential that lies within each and every one of us as I recovered from the stroke. It has taught me to appreciate and celebrate the miracle of life, and to recognise the true power and potential within myself and others.

Journal Prompt: Reflect on the miraculous nature of the human brain and its profound impact on your own life, exploring the ways in which this understanding has deepened your appreciation for the complexities of life, the power within yourself, and the potential for transformation and growth.

9

Thoughts

▮ *You are always at choice with your thoughts; Think about your desired future outcome* ▮

We all have the power to choose our thoughts, and the thoughts we choose have a significant impact on our lives.

Our thoughts shape our beliefs, emotions, and actions, and ultimately determine the outcome of our lives.

The good news is that we always have a choice in what we think about and can choose to focus on thoughts that will lead us towards our desired future outcome.

One of the most effective ways to take control of our thoughts is to become aware of them. This means paying attention to the thoughts that are running through our minds and identifying any negative or limiting thoughts that may be holding us back.

Once we are aware of these thoughts, we can challenge them and replace them with more positive and empowering thoughts.

It's important to remember that we are not always going to have positive thoughts, but it's normal to have negative thoughts from time to time. However, by becoming aware of our negative thoughts, we can choose how much attention we give to them, and we can choose to redirect our thoughts to something positive.

Action Step: Cultivate self-awareness by consciously monitoring your thoughts throughout the day, identifying any negative or limiting patterns, and actively replacing them with positive and empowering thoughts that align with your desired future outcome.

10

Support

People want to help; They want you to win!

Many of us have been taught that the world is a competitive and harsh place, where people are out for themselves. But I've found that, in general, people want to help others and they want to see others succeed.

There are exceptions, of course, but the general tendency is that people want to help others and see them be successful.

When we think about the people in our lives, we often think about the ones who have helped us along the way. Whether it's a family member, a friend, or a mentor, these are the people who have believed in us, encouraged us, and supported us when we needed it most.

It's important to remember that asking for help is not a sign of weakness, it's a sign of strength. It takes courage to admit that we need help and to be vulnerable with others.

When we are open and honest about our needs, we create the opportunity for others to step in and help us. It's also important to remember that people want to help in different ways. Some people may be able to offer practical assistance, while others may offer emotional support.

Also, we can help others in many ways, even in small ways, such as by offering a compliment, a word of encouragement, or a simple act of kindness. As my late father used to say, "It's simple, we're here to help one another."

> Journal Prompt: Reflect on the belief that people generally want to help others and see them succeed, and explore instances in your own life where you have experienced or witnessed acts of support and kindness, recognising the impact these moments have had on your journey and considering how you can continue to foster a culture of helping and supporting others.

11

Celebrate

Mentally celebrate all the wins no matter how big or small

Mentally celebrating all of our wins, no matter how big or small, is an important part of maintaining a positive attitude and staying motivated.

When we take the time to acknowledge and appreciate the progress we've made, it helps us to stay focused on our goals and to continue moving forward.

Small wins, such as completing a task or achieving a minor goal, can often be overlooked or dismissed as insignificant. However, it's important to remember that these small wins are still progress and they are still worth celebrating. They are stepping stones towards achieving our larger goals, and they help to keep us motivated and on track.

Big wins are obviously worth celebrating. They are a clear indication that our beliefs, hard work and dedication are paying off, and they should be recognised and celebrated accordingly. However, it's important to remember that these big wins are built on the foundation of all the small wins that came before them.

Mentally celebrating our wins also helps to boost our confidence and self-esteem. When we take the time to acknowledge and appreciate our achievements, it helps us to feel good about ourselves and to believe in our abilities. This in turn helps us to take on new challenges and to continue making progress towards our goals.

> **Action Step:** Take a few moments each day to reflect on and mentally celebrate your wins, both big and small, expressing gratitude for the progress you have made and the accomplishments you have achieved, reinforcing a positive attitude and motivating yourself to keep moving forward.

12

Positivity

Build a positive mindset

Building a positive mindset is essential for leading a happy and fulfilling life.

It's not always easy to maintain a positive attitude, especially when we're facing challenges or setbacks. However, with a little effort and determination, we can train ourselves to think more positively.

One of the most effective ways to build a positive mindset is to practice gratitude. This means focusing on the things in our lives that we are thankful for, rather than dwelling on the things that are going wrong.

When we shift our focus to the things we are grateful for, it can help to improve our mood and to put our problems into perspective. Look for the things in our lives that we take for granted like waking in the morning to experience another day on planet Earth. This in itself is a miracle and yet we somehow forget just how miraculous that actually is. It is possible to find gratitude in everything.

Another important aspect of building a positive mindset is to surround ourselves with positive people. Being around people who are optimistic, supportive, and encouraging can help to lift our spirits and to keep us motivated. On the other hand, being around negative or critical people can have the opposite effect, so it's important to be mindful of the company we keep.

Journal Prompt: Reflect on the power of gratitude and the impact it can have on your mindset, and write about three things you are grateful for today, no matter how big or small, to cultivate a positive perspective and foster happiness in your life.

13

Receiving

Accept help with gratitude and love

Accepting help with gratitude and love is an important part of being open to support and growth.

When we are open to receiving help, we open ourselves up to new possibilities and opportunities. We can learn new skills, gain new perspectives, and achieve our goals more quickly and efficiently.

It is often difficult to accept help, especially when we are used to doing things on our own or when we believe that accepting help is a sign of weakness. However, accepting help is a sign of strength, it takes courage to admit that we need help and to be vulnerable with others. When we are open and honest about our needs, we create the opportunity for others to step in and help us.

When we accept help, it's important to do so with gratitude and love. Gratitude helps us to appreciate the help we receive and to acknowledge the effort and kindness of the person offering it. Love helps us to approach the situation with an open heart and a positive attitude, it makes it easier to let go of our pride and to accept help with humility.

Action Step: Practice accepting help with gratitude and love by consciously expressing appreciation to those who offer support, and embrace the opportunities for growth and connection that come from allowing others to lend a helping hand.

14

Temporary

Nothing is permanent; Everything is temporary

It's easy to get caught up in fear and worry and to believe that our current circumstances are permanent.

Whether it's a difficult situation or a positive one, it's important to remember that nothing is permanent and everything is temporary. This perspective can help us to better manage our emotions and reactions to events in our lives.

Understanding that nothing is permanent can help us to put things in perspective and to understand that difficult situations will eventually pass.

It can also help us appreciate the good times and make the most of them while they last.

When we understand that everything is temporary, it can help us to let go of things that are holding us back and to make necessary changes.

In addition, the temporary nature of things can also remind us to live in the present moment. We can't change the past or predict the future, but we can make the most of the present. We can focus on what we have and enjoy the present moment, rather than dwelling on what we don't have or what's to come.

Journal Prompt: Reflect on the temporary nature of life and how it can shift your perspective, allowing you to embrace the present moment, appreciate the good times, and navigate difficult situations with the understanding that they too shall pass.

15

Love

Feel the love flowing to you

Feeling the love flowing to us is a powerful way to connect with our inner selves and experience a sense of peace and well-being.

When we allow ourselves to feel the love that is flowing to us, we open ourselves up to the positive energy that surrounds us and we become more receptive to the love that is already present in our lives.

One way to feel the love flowing to us is to practice gratitude. When we focus on the things in our lives that we are thankful for, we shift our attention away from negative thoughts and feelings and towards the positive. As we focus on the things that bring us joy and happiness, we open ourselves up to the love that is already present in our lives.

Another way to feel the love flowing to us is to surround ourselves with positive energy from people who are kind and supportive, or by being in nature, listening to music or taking time to lose ourselves in a good book.

Also, when we take care of our bodies and minds, we create an environment that is conducive to feeling the love flowing to us. This can include things like exercise, healthy eating, and getting enough sleep.

Action Step: Take a few moments each day to consciously tune in to the love that is flowing to you, whether through practicing gratitude, connecting with positive people or activities, or taking care of your physical and mental well-being, and allow yourself to fully experience the peace and well-being that comes with it.

16

Rebuild

Learn and understand how the brain and body re-builds

Learning and understanding how the brain and body rebuilds is essential for maintaining optimal physical and mental health and therefore becomes the foundation for any transformation.

The process of rebuilding involves the repair and regeneration of damaged cells, tissues, and organs. This natural process occurs throughout our lives, and it's essential for maintaining our overall well-being.

The brain is a complex organ that is responsible for controlling many of our bodily functions. It's made up of billions of neurons, which are the cells responsible for transmitting information throughout the brain and body. When neurons are damaged, the brain is able to repair and rebuild them through a process called neurogenesis. This process involves the growth and development of new neurons, which helps to maintain the brain's ability to function properly.

Additionally, the body is able to rebuild itself through a process called tissue repair. This process involves the repair and regeneration of damaged cells, tissues, and organs. The body is able to repair itself through the growth and development of new cells, as well as through the removal of damaged or dead cells. Even a basic understanding of this knowledge was instrumental in my recovery from stroke and applies to all of us in any transformative situation.

> **Journal Prompt:** Reflect on the remarkable process of rebuilding and regeneration that occurs in the brain and body, and consider how this understanding can empower you to prioritise your physical and mental health as the foundation for any transformative journey.

17

Gratitude

Be grateful for what you have, and don't dwell on lack or loss

Being grateful for what we have, and not dwelling on lack or loss, is an essential part of maintaining a positive attitude and leading a fulfilling life.

When we focus on the things we are thankful for, we shift our attention away from negative thoughts and feelings and towards the positive. This helps us to appreciate the good things in our lives and to be content with what we have.

The phrase 'Be grateful for what you have, and don't dwell on lack or loss' serves as a powerful tool for personal transformation. It encourages us to shift our focus from what we lack or have lost to what we currently have in our lives.

Gratitude is a positive emotion that can boost one's mental and emotional well-being. When we adopt a grateful mindset, we cultivate a greater sense of happiness and contentment in our lives.

This shift in perspective can lead to personal transformation by allowing us to appreciate what we have and focus on opportunities for growth and development, instead of dwelling on our shortcomings.

Action Step: Take a few moments each day to practice gratitude by consciously acknowledging and appreciating the things you are thankful for, shifting your focus from lack or loss to the abundance and blessings in your life.

18

Nature

Get outside in nature, breathe in the fresh air;
listen to the birds; and feel the connection with
Mother Earth

Engaging in activities such as getting outside in nature, breathing in the fresh air, listening to the birds, and feeling the connection with Mother Earth can have a profound impact on our physical and mental well-being.

Nature has a way of grounding us, calming our minds, and reminding us of our place in the world.

Spending time in nature can help to reduce stress and improve our mood. The sights, sounds and smells of nature can have a calming effect on the mind, helping to reduce feelings of anxiety and depression. Being surrounded by trees, plants and wildlife can help us to feel more connected to the world around us, boosting our self-esteem and reducing feelings of isolation.

From a physical perspective, breathing in the fresh air can help to improve our lung function, reduce inflammation and boost the immune system. The natural setting of nature can help to reduce the level of pollutants in the air, allowing us to take in cleaner and fresher air into our lungs.

Being in nature provides a sense of peace and calm that is emotionally and spiritually restorative and feeling the connection with Mother Earth can remind us of our place in the world and the interconnectedness of all living things. It can help us to feel more grounded, connected and in tune with the universe.

Journal Prompt: Take a moment to reflect on the impact of nature on your well-being and write about a specific experience or activity in nature that has had a profound effect on your physical and mental state.

19

Judgement II

> *Try not to judge a situation as either good or bad, it is just an experience and nothing more. Judging a situation just causes unnecessary unease in the body*

Trying not to judge a situation as either good or bad, and seeing it as just an experience, can help to reduce unnecessary tension in the body.

Judgement creates an emotional response that can be either positive or negative, and this can affect our mental and physical well-being.

Labelling a situation as good or bad can create biases that

prevent us from understanding the situation objectively. It can impair our ability to think critically and make sound decisions. It can also cause us to react emotionally instead of responding in a grounded calm manner.

When we judge a situation as bad, it creates negative emotions such as stress, anger and frustration. These negative emotions can lead to physical symptoms such as headaches, fatigue, and muscle tension. On the other hand, when we judge a situation as good, it can create positive emotions such as happiness and excitement, but it can also create unrealistic expectations that can lead to disappointment.

It's important to remember that every situation, whether it is perceived as good or bad, is just an experience. It's something that happened and it's something that we can learn from. The experience itself, may not be good or bad, but it can be the way we perceive it that can make it so.

Action Step: Practice non-judgment by consciously refraining from labelling situations as good or bad, and instead, focus on observing and accepting them as neutral experiences, allowing yourself to release unnecessary tension in the body and cultivate a more balanced perspective.

20

Gratitude II

Change your habits: Swap judgement for gratitude ▮

Changing our habits can have a profound impact on our lives. One habit that can be particularly beneficial to change is swapping judgement for gratitude.

Instead of focusing on what's wrong or what's missing in our lives, we can shift our attention to what we are grateful for.

Gratitude is the practice of being thankful for what we have, instead of dwelling on what we don't have. It's a powerful tool that can help us to appreciate the good things in our lives. When we focus on gratitude, we shift our attention away from negative thoughts and feelings and towards the positive.

Swapping judgement for gratitude can also have a positive impact on our mental and physical well-being. It can help to reduce stress and improve our mood, by promoting feelings of positivity and contentment. It can also boost our self-esteem and self-worth, by helping us to feel good about ourselves and to believe in our abilities.

One way to begin swapping judgement for gratitude is to start a gratitude journal. Every day, write down 3 things you're grateful for, no matter how small. This can be things like the taste of your morning coffee, the warmth of the sun on your skin or the kindness of a friend. Reflecting on what we're grateful for on a daily basis can help to create a habit of gratitude.

Journal Prompt: Reflect on the transformative power of swapping judgement for gratitude in your life and explore how cultivating a daily gratitude practice can positively shift your mindset and enhance your overall well-being.

21

Focus

> *If you've experienced a setback in your life, don't compare your former life with your current situation; It's a pointless waste of energy that will hinder your transformation. Instead, use your energy to focus on love and your future self*

Experiencing a setback in life can be difficult and it's natural to compare our current situation to our former life.

However, comparing our former life with our current situation is a pointless waste of energy that can hinder our transformation (or recovery or comeback). It can make us feel stuck in the past and prevent us from moving forward.

When we focus on the past, we are unable to see the opportunities that are available to us in the present. We are unable to see the potential for growth and change.

Comparing our current situation to our former life can make us feel like we've lost something and that we can never get it back. This can lead to feelings of sadness, frustration and disappointment.

Instead of comparing our former life with our current situation, we should use our energy to focus on love and our future self. Love is the foundation for growth and change. It allows us to see the potential for growth and change in our lives. It also helps us to see the good in ourselves and in others.

When we focus on our future self, we are able to see the potential for growth and change in our lives. We are able to see the possibilities that are available to us. We are able to see the potential for a better future

Action Step: Shift your focus from comparing your former life to your current situation and instead channel your energy towards cultivating self-love and envisioning a positive future for yourself, allowing space for growth and embracing new possibilities.

22

Move

> *Move your body. Do whatever you can. It might be*
> *small but anything is better than nothing. Your body*
> *is your vessel carrying you on your journey on planet*
> *Earth so nurture it and love it*

Moving our bodies is essential for maintaining optimal physical and mental health.

It's a powerful way to reduce stress, improve our mood, and boost our overall well-being. Our body is our vessel, carrying us on our journey on planet Earth, so it's essential to nurture and love it.

Getting caught up in our daily routines and neglecting our

physical health is easy, but even small movements can make a big difference. Taking a walk around the block, stretching, or doing a few minutes of yoga can help to increase blood flow, reduce muscle tension, and boost our energy levels.

Physical activity can also have a positive impact on our mental health. It releases endorphins, the chemicals in the brain that act as natural painkillers and mood elevators.

Regular exercise can also improve our sleep, which is essential for maintaining good mental health.

It's important to remember that anything is better than nothing. Even if you can't commit to a regular exercise routine, there are small things you can do to move your body throughout the day. Take the stairs instead of the elevator, walk or bike to work, or simply stand up and stretch every hour.

> **Journal Prompt:** Reflect on the ways in which you can incorporate more movement into your daily life, whether it's through exercise routines, active hobbies, or small actions, and explore the impact it has on your physical and mental well-being.

23

Emotions

Develop an advanced emotional intelligence

Developing advanced emotional intelligence is essential for leading a fulfilling and successful life. Emotional intelligence is the ability to understand, manage, and use our emotions effectively.

During any transformation, it is normal to come up against challenges that cause an emotional reaction. I recall that in the first 6 months of my recovery from stroke, I faced great sadness and anger towards the situation and the circumstances in which I found myself. The emotions were off the scale, so mastery of emotions was something that I had to work on and still do to this day; it's a never-ending process.

Emotional intelligence is composed of several key components, including emotional awareness, empathy, emotional regulation, and social skills; taking this to an advanced level includes the ability to heal past emotional trauma in oneself coupled with an ability to feel an emotion without adding any associated meaning. The latter of these advanced levels means being able to feel an emotion (e.g. sadness) yet not adding any specific meaning or cause for that emotion (e.g. I feel sad because of 'XYZ').

Emotions also provide an indicator of alignment with our source energy, or our inner self. Whenever we feel "off" it is often a sign that we have built up resistance from our inner self. The secret to restoring that alignment is self-love and self-compassion.

To develop advanced emotional intelligence, it is important to practice self-reflection and self-awareness. This means taking the time to understand our emotions, the triggers that cause them, and how we react to them.

> **Action Step**: Take time each day for self-reflection and self-awareness, observing your emotions, their triggers, and your reactions to them without attaching specific meaning, allowing yourself to cultivate advanced emotional intelligence.

24

Present

Transformation will be stronger when you allow your-self to ease into the flow which might mean accep-tance of the long road, slowing down tasks and getting plenty of restorative sleep

Transformation is a process that involves change and growth, and it can be a challenging and difficult journey.

However, it is important to remember that the process can be made stronger when you allow yourself to ease into the flow. This means accepting that the road to transformation may be long and winding and that it is okay to take your time and not rush through the process.

One way to ease into the flow is by slowing down tasks and being mindful of the present moment. This means not trying to rush through things and instead taking the time to fully engage with the task at hand. This can help to reduce stress and increase productivity, as well as helping to foster a sense of calm and clarity.

Another important aspect of easing into the flow is getting plenty of restorative sleep. Sleep is essential for both physical and mental well-being, and it is important to make sure that you are getting enough quality sleep each night. This can be achieved by creating a bedtime routine, avoiding screens before bed, and creating a comfortable sleeping environment.

Journal Prompt: How can you embrace the process of transformation by easing into the flow and allowing yourself to take the necessary time and rest to support your journey?

Vision

Having set the vision, break it down into incremental goals and see yourself achieving those goals, and before you know it, your vision starts to become your reality

Having a clear vision is the first step towards achieving success. It is essential to know what you want to achieve and to have a clear understanding of the end goal.

However, setting a vision is just the beginning, and it's essential to break it down into incremental goals. This will help to make the vision more manageable and achievable.

Breaking down the vision into smaller, incremental goals helps to create a sense of progress. It allows you to see the small victories that you achieve along the way, which can help to keep you motivated and on track towards achieving the overall vision. Each small goal that you achieve is a step towards the bigger picture, and it helps to build momentum.

It's also important to visualise yourself achieving those goals. This technique is known as visualisation and it's a powerful tool to help you achieve your goals. By picturing yourself achieving your goals in your mind, you are training your brain to believe that it's possible. This helps to increase your motivation, and it also helps you to be better prepared for when the opportunity presents itself.

Action step: Break down your clear vision into incremental goals and regularly visualize yourself achieving them to maintain motivation and build momentum towards your ultimate success.

26

Journey

> *The richness of the experience is in the journey and not the destination*

The journey of life is full of ups and downs, twists and turns, and it can be easy to get caught up in the destination.

We often focus on reaching our goals, and achieving success, without taking the time to appreciate the journey. However, the richness of the experience is not in the destination, but in the journey.

The journey is where we learn, grow, and develop. It's where we make mistakes and learn from them. It's where we meet new people and build relationships. It's where we discover our passions and interests. The journey is where we find out who we are and what we are capable of. The destination is simply a byproduct of the journey.

When we focus too much on the destination, we can miss out on the beauty and richness of the journey. We may rush through the process, missing out on the small moments and experiences that make life worth living. By focusing on the journey, we can appreciate the present, and be grateful for the experiences that come our way.

Journal prompt: Take a moment to reflect on your journey in life and the lessons, growth, and experiences it has brought you. What are some of the memorable moments and valuable insights you have gained along the way?

27

Balance

Learn to balance determination with surrender to remove internal resistance to transformation

Transformation is a process that requires determination and perseverance, but it is also important to learn to balance determination with surrender.

This balance can help to remove internal resistance to transformation and make the process more smooth and effective.

Determination is important because it gives us the drive and motivation to achieve our goals. It helps us to focus on our vision and to take action towards achieving it. Without determination, we may lack the willpower to make the necessary changes in our lives.

Surrender, on the other hand, is about letting go of control and accepting what is. It is about being open to new possibilities and trusting that things will work out in the end. Surrender helps to remove internal resistance because it allows us to accept and work with the current situation, rather than fighting against it.

When we combine determination with surrender, we create a powerful balance. Determination gives us the drive to move forward, and surrender helps us to let go of resistance and accept the present moment. This balance allows us to take action towards our goals while also being open to new opportunities and possibilities.

Action step: Practice finding the balance between determination and surrender by setting clear goals and taking consistent action towards them, while also practicing acceptance, letting go of control, and being open to the flow of life.

28

Comfort Zone

*Step out of your comfort zone. Your comfort zone
will only keep you trapped where you are*

Stepping out of your comfort zone can be a difficult and daunting task, but it is also an essential step towards growth and development.

Your comfort zone is the place where you feel safe and secure, but it can also be a trap that keeps you stuck and prevents you from reaching your full potential.

When you step out of your comfort zone, you open yourself up to new opportunities and experiences. You challenge yourself to grow and develop, and you learn to adapt to new situations. This helps to build confidence and resilience, which can be beneficial in all aspects of life.

Stepping out of your comfort zone also allows you to discover new things about yourself. You may find that you have untapped talents and abilities, and you may be able to achieve things you never thought possible.

It's important to remember that stepping out of your comfort zone doesn't have to be a big, dramatic change. It can be small steps, like trying new foods or taking a different route to work. It's about pushing yourself to try new things and not being limited by your fears or doubts.

Journal Prompt: Reflect on a recent experience where you stepped out of your comfort zone, big or small. How did it make you feel? What did you learn about yourself through this experience?

29

Nature II

Get outside and walk in nature if possible. Consider playing your favourite playlist for accompaniment

Walking in nature can be an incredibly uplifting and rejuvenating experience. The natural world offers an abundance of beauty, tranquillity and a sense of connection to something greater than oneself.

As I had to learn to walk again after the stroke, it was something that I was determined to do as I intuitively knew that being able to 'get out' in nature would propel my recovery and personal transformation. I would also play very gentle and soothing music to accompany my walks.

There are many benefits to walking in nature. Firstly, it can be a great way to get some exercise and fresh air. Being active and spending time outdoors has been shown to positively affect physical health such as reducing the risk of heart disease, diabetes, and obesity.

Additionally, walking in nature can also help to improve mental health by reducing symptoms of depression, anxiety and stress. It can also improve mood and cognitive function and has been found to enhance creativity and productivity.

It is also the opportunity to connect with the natural world, which can remind us of the beauty and fragility of life and it can help to put things into perspective.

Furthermore, it serves as a poignant reminder of the cyclical nature of life, where we witness the perpetual renewal and transformation mirrored in the ever-changing seasons.

Action Step: Make a commitment to incorporate regular walks in nature into your routine, even if it's just for a few minutes each day. Notice how it uplifts your mood, rejuvenates your energy, and provides a sense of connection with the natural world.

30

Nature III

Observe the wonder of nature wherever you can. It reflects the pure natural state of continuous growth and recovery throughout the seasons

Nature is a powerful and ever-changing force; observing its wonder can be a profound and transformative experience.

The natural world reflects the pure natural state of continuous growth and recovery throughout the seasons. It is a reminder of the cyclical nature of life and the resilience of the earth when we leave Mother Earth to tend to herself.

By observing nature, we can learn to appreciate the beauty of the world around us. The colours, textures, and patterns of nature are endlessly fascinating and can provide a sense of awe and wonder. The natural world can also be a source of inspiration and it can be a reminder of the beauty of immense complexity that is made to appear seemingly simple. Being in nature releases the peace within us. Have you noticed how peaceful you feel when wandering alone in nature?

Nature also teaches us about the importance of growth and recovery. The changing of the seasons is a reminder that life is a continuous cycle of growth and decay. We can learn to embrace change and understand that evolution is not always linear. Nature teaches us that it's okay to take a step back and to recover, that it's all part of the process.

Observing nature can also be a way to connect with the earth and appreciate the interdependence of all living things. It can remind us of our place in the world and the impact we have on the environment.

Journal Prompt: Take a moment to immerse yourself in nature and reflect on its profound impact on your senses and emotions. How does observing the wonders of nature inspire you, teach you about growth and recovery, and deepen your connection to the world around you?

31

Habits

*If you are able, walk outside as often as possible,
ideally at least twice a day if you can*

Walking outside is one of the simplest and most beneficial things we can do for our overall health and well-being. Not only does it provide physical benefits such as increased cardio-vascular fitness and muscle strength, but it also has a positive impact on our mental health.

Studies have shown that spending time in nature can reduce stress and anxiety, improve mood, and even boost cognitive function. Additionally, walking outside can help us to get some much-needed fresh air and sunlight, both of which are essential for maintaining a healthy immune system.

It is recommended that adults aim to get at least 30 minutes of moderate-intensity physical activity each day, and walking is a great way to do this. Walking briskly can raise your heart rate and breathing, which can help to improve cardiovascular fitness. Additionally, walking on uneven surfaces such as dirt paths or gravel can also help to improve balance and leg strength.

If you are able, try to walk outside as often as possible, ideally at least twice a day. This can be a great way to fit in regular physical activity while also getting the benefits of spending time in nature. Try to make it a habit by setting aside specific times of day to go for a walk, such as early morning, during your lunch break or before bed.

For those who find it physically difficult to walk, try to get outside on a regular basis. I recall when I was recovering from the stroke, I had to create the new habit of walking every day even when I could only shuffle along and make 200 yards before intense fatigue would take over. Make a commitment whatever your present condition.

Action Step: Commit to incorporating outdoor walks into your daily routine by scheduling dedicated time slots for brisk walks in nature, aiming for at least 30 minutes each session, and making it a habit to walk outside at least twice a day for the physical and mental health benefits it offers.

32

Destiny

Take control of your destiny and never be afraid of mixing up the set plan. You are always in control!

Taking control of your own destiny is about being proactive and making decisions that will shape your future.

It means being confident in your ability to navigate life's challenges and opportunities and being willing to take risks in pursuit of your goals. It also means being open to change and being willing to adjust your plans as necessary to achieve your desired outcome.

One of the keys to taking control of your own destiny is to never be afraid of mixing up the set plan. Life is unpredictable, and things don't always go as planned. Instead of feeling defeated by setbacks or obstacles, view them as opportunities to learn and grow. Be open to new possibilities and be willing to take a different approach if your current plan isn't working.

Another important aspect of taking control of your own destiny is to take responsibility for your actions. This means acknowledging that the choices you make have a direct impact on your life and accepting the consequences of those choices. It also means being accountable for your own happiness and well-being and not relying on others to provide it for you.

It is important to remember that you are always in control of your own destiny. You have the power to make decisions that will shape your future and take action to achieve your goals.

Journal Prompt: Reflect on a time when you took control of your own destiny by making proactive decisions and embracing change. How did this experience shape your future, and what did you learn about yourself in the process?

33

Possibilities

Try not to focus on the loss of your former self, but rather, switch your focus on the possibilities and potentialities held within transformation

Transformation can be a difficult process, especially when it involves the loss of our former self.

We may feel like we are losing a part of ourselves or that we are no longer the person we used to be. However, it is important to remember that transformation is not only about loss but also about gain.

Instead of focusing on the loss of your former self, try to shift your focus to the possibilities and potentialities held within transformation.

Transformation is an opportunity for growth and change, and it can open up new doors and possibilities for you. It can help you to discover new parts of yourself and to develop new skills and abilities.

Transformation is also an opportunity to break out of old patterns and to create a new life for yourself. It can help you to let go of limiting beliefs and to create new ways of thinking and being. It can also help you to move past old traumas and to create a more fulfilling life for yourself.

It is important to remember that transformation is not a one-time event, it is a continuous process. It is ongoing and it's not always easy. It's natural to feel scared, lost or confused, but it's important to keep in mind that it's all part of the process.

Action Step: Embrace the process of transformation by focusing on the possibilities and potentialities it holds, and remind yourself that it's a continuous journey of growth and change.

34

Tools

Use tools to help you with carrying out multiple tasks at once so that you give your transforming brain a fighting chance. It also reduces any additional pressure and stress

In our modern world, it's not uncommon to find ourselves juggling multiple tasks at once. Whether it's work, family, or personal responsibilities, it can be overwhelming to try and keep up with everything.

However, using tools to help you carry out multiple tasks can give your transforming brain a fighting chance and also reduce additional pressure and stress.

One helpful tool is a calendar or scheduling app. This can help you to keep track of your deadlines, appointments, and to-do lists. It can also help you to prioritise your tasks and to plan your time more effectively.

Another helpful tool is a note-taking app, which can help you to organise your thoughts and ideas, and to keep track of important information.

Another tool that can be useful is an approach to time management which involves breaking your work into short, focused intervals, separated by short breaks. This can help you to stay focused and productive throughout the day and to avoid burnout.

In addition, tools such as meditation apps or stress management apps can help you reduce stress and maintain a healthy mindset while you are working on multiple tasks.

Journal Prompt: Reflect on the tools and strategies you currently use or could implement to help manage multiple tasks and responsibilities in your daily life, and how they contribute to reducing overwhelm and maintaining productivity.

35

Comparison

> *Give up all fear-based comparisons of your former self with your current transforming self. The comparison could cause you to hold an unhealthy self-image and cause self-judgment of your transforming self*

Comparison is a natural human tendency, but when it comes to our own personal growth and transformation, it can be detrimental.

Giving up fear-based comparisons of our former self with our current transforming self is essential for our well-being and self-acceptance.

When we compare our former self to our current self, we may focus on what we think we lack or what we are not yet able to do, and this can cause us to hold an unhealthy self-image and self-judgment. This can lead to feelings of inadequacy and self-doubt which can slow down or even halt our personal growth and transformation.

It's an overused cliche, but it's important to remember that "transformation is a journey, not a destination". We are constantly growing and changing, and it's important to embrace where we are in the present moment. It's important to focus on the progress we have made, rather than dwelling on what we haven't yet achieved.

It's also important to remember that everyone's journey is different. We all have our own unique paths to follow and comparison with others can be unhealthy. We should give ourselves credit for the progress we've made, no matter how small it may seem.

Action Step: Practice self-compassion and celebrate your own progress and growth, embracing the uniqueness of your own journey without comparing it to others.

36

Letting Go

> *Allow old emotions to pass through the body without attaching any meaning or judgment. Holding on to past trauma and associated emotions can lead to dis-ease*

Emotions are an important part of being human and they can be powerful forces that shape our thoughts and behaviours, and how we experience the world.

However, when it comes to past traumas and negative emotions, it's important to allow them to pass through the body without attaching any meaning or judgment.

Holding onto past traumas and associated emotions can lead to disease (or as I like to write it, dis-ease, to represent the lack of ease within the body), both physically and mentally.

When we attach meaning or judgment to our emotions, we can become stuck in them, and they can start to control our thoughts and behaviours. This can lead to negative patterns of thinking and feeling, which can manifest as physical and mental health problems.

Try to allow old emotions to pass through the body, without clinging to them or pushing them away. Just observe them with a non-judgmental attitude. This can be difficult, but with practice, it can become easier.

Ways to do this include mindfulness practices such as meditation or yoga, or through writing, art, music, or talking to a coach or therapist. These practices can help to increase awareness and acceptance of our emotions and to develop a non-judgmental attitude towards them.

> Journal Prompt: Reflect on your relationship with past traumas and negative emotions. How can you practice allowing them to pass through your body without attaching meaning or judgment, and what strategies can you implement to cultivate a non-judgmental attitude towards your emotions?

37

Discovery

Allow yourself to explore new interests without any judgment if you wish to move on and explore some-thing else. Life is all about experiences and exploring what we want to pursue

Exploring new interests is an important part of personal growth and self-discovery. It allows us to expand our knowledge, skills, and experiences, and to find new passions and hobbies.

If we wish to move on and explore something else, then we should feel free to do so without any self-judgement.

Life is all about experiences and exploring what we want to

pursue. It's important to remember that our interests and passions can change over time and that's okay. We should not feel guilty or ashamed for wanting to explore something new or for moving on from a previous interest.

When we are open to new experiences, we are also open to new opportunities and possibilities. We never know what we might discover or where it might lead us.

It's important to be open and willing to try new things, even if we're not sure if it's something we'll like or stick with.

It's also important to remember that it's okay to fail. Failure is a natural part of the learning and exploration process. It's not a failure if we learn something from it.

> **Action Step:** Take a step towards exploring a new interest or passion without any self-judgment. Allow yourself to be open to new experiences and embrace the possibility of discovering something new about yourself.

38

Habits II

Transformation might require following new routines. Don't be dismissive of new transformative habits

Transformation often requires following new routines and habits. This can be challenging and can take time to adjust to, but it is essential for achieving the desired change.

When embarking on a transformative journey, it's important not to dismiss new habits and routines out of hand.

New habits can be difficult to form, but they are the key to achieving our goals and making lasting change. Our brains are wired to resist change, but with persistence, we can rewire our brains to accept new habits and routines.

It's important to understand that change can take time and that progress is not always linear. There might be setbacks and obstacles along the way, but it's important to keep going and not give up.

It's also important to be flexible and open to new ways of doing things. The way we used to do things may not be the best way for our current situation or goals.

In addition, it's important to be mindful of the reasons behind our new habits and routines. It's easy to fall into the trap of following new habits without really understanding why we are doing them. By being mindful of our motivations, we can ensure that our new habits align with our values and goals.

Journal Prompt: Reflect on the new routines and habits you have incorporated into your life as part of your transformative journey. How have they challenged you, and what adjustments have you made along the way?

39

Perspective

Perspective is a powerful tool, learn to become a master of perspective and observe the world from multiple viewpoints for it will serve you well

Perspective is a powerful tool that can shape the way we see and understand the world around us. It can also shape the way we see and understand ourselves.

Learning to become a master of perspective and observing the world from multiple viewpoints can serve us well in many aspects of our lives.

One of the key benefits of having a diverse perspective is

that it can help us to understand and empathise with others. When we are able to see things from multiple viewpoints, we can better understand the motivations and actions of those around us. This can lead to more meaningful connections and relationships, and can also help us to navigate conflicts and misunderstandings.

Another benefit of having a diverse perspective is that it can help us to make better decisions. When we are able to see things from multiple viewpoints, we can consider different options and weigh the pros and cons of each. This can lead to more informed and thoughtful decisions.

Having a diverse perspective can also help us to be more creative. When we are able to see things from different angles, we can come up with new and unique ideas. It can also help us to solve problems more effectively.

Action Step: Practice expanding your perspective by intentionally seeking out different viewpoints and opinions. Engage in conversations with people who have diverse backgrounds and experiences, read books or articles from different perspectives, and challenge your own assumptions and biases.

40

Empowerment

> *When circumstances seem to give you a rough hand,*
> *rather than playing the victim, adopt a sense of the*
> *"bigger picture". Move to a perspective of this*
> *happened for me and not to me.*

If it seems that life has dealt us a rough hand, it can be easy to fall into the trap of feeling like a victim. We may feel like we are at the mercy of our circumstances and that we have no control over what happens to us.

However, adopting a sense of the "bigger picture" can help us to shift our perspective and to see our challenges as opportunities for growth and change.

When we move to a perspective of "this happened for me and not to me," we start to see our challenges as opportunities for personal development. We understand that these challenges are not happening to us but rather they are happening for us. They are helping us to grow and become stronger.

This perspective also allows us to take responsibility for our own lives and to take action to improve our circumstances. Instead of feeling helpless and powerless, we become empowered and take control of our own lives. It's important to remember that our challenges are not permanent. They are temporary and will pass.

We may not know the reason why certain things happen to us, but we can trust that everything happens for a reason. We can trust that the universe always has our best interests at heart, even if the circumstances appear anything but appealing at the time.

Journal Prompt: Reflect on a difficult situation or challenge you have faced in your life. How might adopting a perspective of "this happened for me and not to me" shift your understanding of that experience? How could this perspective empower you to take control of your own growth and create positive change?

41

Gratitude III

> *Always look for gratitude in anything when the chips are down. Gratitude helps lift a mood to a higher frequency*

In times of adversity, it can be easy to focus on the negative and to let ourselves be consumed by negative thoughts and emotions.

However, looking for gratitude in anything can help to lift our mood to a higher frequency. Gratitude is a powerful tool that can change our perspective and help us to see the positive in difficult situations.

Practicing gratitude can help us to shift our focus from what we lack to what we have. It helps us to appreciate the good things in our lives, no matter how small they may be. This can help to improve our overall well-being and to increase our sense of happiness and contentment.

Try to practice gratitude for the aspects of life that we often take for granted, like the ability to sense the world around us or for the opportunity to experience life for another day after waking from a night's sleep or for a restful night's sleep itself. When you explore all the reasons to be grateful it soon becomes apparent that the list of reasons is endless.

Gratitude can also help to reduce stress and anxiety. When we focus on the things we are grateful for, we are less likely to ruminate on negative thoughts and emotions. It helps us to shift our focus away from negative thoughts, and to see the bigger picture.

Action Step: Start a gratitude practice by taking a few minutes each day to reflect on and write down three things you are grateful for. Focus on the small, every-day blessings that often go unnoticed. This practice can help shift your mindset and cultivate a sense of appreciation even in challenging times.

42

Thoughts II

> *Everything is created in the mind through thought.*
> *We can think negatively and let fear and doubt*
> *dominate our thoughts, or we can think positively*
> *and let our imagination paint a picture of what we*
> *desire on the screen of our mind. We are always at*
> *choice how we think.*

It's true that everything is created in the mind through thought.

Our thoughts have the power to shape our reality and influence our actions and decisions. This is why it is important to be mindful of the thoughts that we allow to dominate our minds.

We have the choice to think negatively and let fear and doubt dominate our thoughts, or we can choose to think positively and let our imagination paint a picture of what we desire on the screen of our minds.

Negative thoughts can hold us back and prevent us from reaching our full potential, while positive thoughts can open up new possibilities and opportunities.

When we focus on positive thoughts, we are able to see the potential in ourselves and in our surroundings. We are able to let go of limiting beliefs and see the world in a more optimistic light. This can help us to achieve our goals, to build better relationships and to find more joy and fulfilment in life.

We can also use our imagination to visualise the life we want to create. By regularly visualising our goals, we can start to see ourselves living the life we desire, and this can help us to take the necessary steps to make it a reality.

Journal Prompt: Explore the power of your thoughts and how they can shape your reality. How can you cultivate a positive mindset and harness the potential of your thoughts to create the life you desire?

43

Flow

> *Get into your flow. Achieving the flow state can unlock all manner of possibilities of personal transformation.*

The concept of "flow state" refers to a mental state in which one is fully absorbed and engaged in an activity, leading to optimal performance and a sense of effortless accomplishment.

Achieving this state can unlock all manner of possibilities for personal transformation.

When we are in the flow state, we are fully present in the moment and our attention is completely focused on the task at hand. We are not easily distracted by external factors and our performance is enhanced. This state of mind can lead to increased productivity, creativity and satisfaction in what we do.

To achieve a flow state, it's important to find activities that are challenging but not overwhelming. Engaging in an activity that is too easy will lead to boredom, while an activity that is too difficult will lead to frustration. Finding the sweet spot in-between, where the activity is just challenging enough to be engaging, is key to achieving a flow state.

Another important factor is to have clear goals and feedback. Having a clear idea of what you want to achieve and how you will measure your progress can help to keep you focused and motivated. Achieving a "state of flow" is another way of allowing the continuous stream of love and well-being to enrich our life experience. It feels good.

Action Step: Identify an activity that you enjoy and find challenging, and create a conducive environment that minimises distractions. Engage in the activity with clear goals and periodically evaluate your progress to help achieve a flow state and unlock your full potential.

44

Relax

> *Let go of stuff that doesn't serve your transformation. Learn to laugh at yourself. Be kind to yourself.*

Transformation often requires letting go of things that don't serve us. This can be difficult, as we may have attachments to certain things, whether it be possessions, relationships, or even old habits and patterns of thinking.

However, it's important to understand that letting go of these things can open up space for new possibilities and opportunities.

One of the best ways to let go of things that don't serve our transformation is to learn to laugh at ourselves. When we can laugh at ourselves, we can see the humour in our own mistakes and setbacks. This can help to put things into perspective and to see that they are not as serious as they may seem.

It's also important to be kind to ourselves. When we are going through a transformative process, it can be easy to be hard on ourselves and beat ourselves up for not being perfect.

However, it's important to remember that we are all human and that we are all doing the best we can. Being kind to ourselves can help to reduce stress and anxiety, and it can also help to improve our overall well-being.

> Journal Prompt: Reflect on a situation or aspect of your life that you may be holding onto but no longer serves your growth. Explore how embracing humour and kindness towards yourself can help you let go and create space for new possibilities and opportunities.

45

Thoughts III

> *Put all your thought energy into your future vision*
> *and let thoughts based on fear and doubt pass*
> *through your mind without attachment or meaning.*
> *Both types of thoughts will create.*

Our thoughts can shape our reality, and it's important to be mindful of the thoughts we allow to dominate. In the pursuit of personal transformation, dedicating our thought energy to visualising a compelling future is paramount.

It also means gracefully allowing thoughts rooted in fear and doubt to pass through without attachment and meaning.

By intentionally centring our attention on the envisioned

transformation, we not only unleash the hidden potential within ourselves and our surroundings but also break free from limiting beliefs. This positive outlook, permeated with joy and positivity, acts as a driving force, propelling us toward our goals and the desired transformation. In essence, it opens the floodgates to abundance, serving as the key to inviting more of everything into our lives.

Conversely, thoughts entwined with fear and doubt can impede our journey. When these negative thoughts and feelings arise, adopting an observant, non-judgmental stance will defuse their power. At first, this is challenging but with practice, this skill can become more attainable.

Crucially, it is not the negative thoughts themselves but the accompanying feelings that create barriers to transformation.

With this insight, when faced with fear, consciously redirect attention to gratitude, joy, and happiness. This will foster progress towards your transformation.

Action Step: Practice redirecting your thoughts towards your future vision and goals, letting go of fear-based thoughts.

46

Worthiness

You were born worthy.

This means that you are inherently valuable and deserving of love and respect, simply because you exist.

Your worthiness is not dependent on your achievements, your appearance, or your possessions. It is an inherent part of who you are.

Unfortunately, many of us have been taught to believe that our worth is dependent on external factors such as our success, our looks, or our possessions. This can lead to feelings of inadequacy and self-doubt.

It's important to remember that you were born worthy. Your worth is not something that you have to earn or prove. It is something that you already possess. You are worthy of love, respect, and happiness, simply because you exist.

It's also important to remember that your worthiness is not dependent on the opinions of others. The opinions of others can be influenced by their own biases and insecurities, and should not be taken as the ultimate truth. The only opinion that truly matters is your own.

> **Action Step**: Practice self-compassion and self-care by engaging in activities that nourish your mind, body, and soul, reinforcing your inherent worthiness and cultivating a strong sense of self-value.

47

Vision II

When you experience a vision for your future it is like peering through a hole in time. Your current reality may not reflect that vision but at all times you have a choice of where to focus your energy. Do you focus on the current reality or do you focus on making your vision your reality?

When we experience a vision for our future, it is like we are peering through a hole in time. The vision we have for ourselves may not reflect our current reality, but it is important to remember that we always have a choice of where to focus our energy.

One option is to focus on our current reality, accepting

it as it is and not reaching for something better. However, this can lead to feeling unfulfilled and stuck in our current circumstances. In fact, feelings of being stuck will result in being stuck.

Another option is to focus on making our vision our reality. This means dedicating time and energy towards turning our vision into a reality, despite the challenges and obstacles that may come our way. It requires work, perseverance, self-compassion and most of all, a positive mental attitude which creates a positive emotional charge of energy.

When we focus on making our vision our reality, it can be easy to get discouraged when things don't happen as quickly as we want them to or when we face obstacles, and this can create feelings of despair and anxiety.

It's important to remember that progress can take time and that setbacks might be part of the process. When setbacks occur don't give up, have grace for yourself and be kind to yourself. On the difficult days just try to do any small thing towards bringing that vision of the future into your reality; it doesn't have to be huge, just a small incremental step that makes you feel good.

> Journal Prompt: Reflect on your vision for the future and explore the small incremental steps you can take today to bring that vision closer to reality while practicing self-compassion and maintaining a positive attitude throughout the journey.

48

Fear

> *"Feel the fear and do it anyway" is a well-known phrase that plays out in our lives all the time. You will know in your heart when the fear and danger is real or not. Don't let the ego-mind-created fear stop you from experiencing the joy of the moment.*

"Feel the fear and do it anyway" is a powerful phrase that encourages us to push through our fears and take action despite the perceived danger.

In many cases, the fear that we feel is not a real danger, but rather a creation of our own mind. The ego mind, in an effort to protect us, can create fears that hold us back from experiencing the joy and excitement of new experiences.

However, it is important to recognise that there are times when fear is a real warning of danger. In these situations, it is important to listen to that warning and take appropriate action.

The key is to be able to distinguish between real and imagined fears.

When the fear is imagined, it is important to continue forward. This is where the phrase "feel the fear and do it anyway" comes into play. The word 'fear' can form an interesting acronym; False Evidence Appearing Real. When the fear is imagined try to remember this acronym as it might help create the necessary motivation to move despite the feeling of fear.

By acknowledging the fear and moving forward despite it, we can experience the joy and excitement of new experiences.

Action Step: Identify one fear that is holding you back and challenge yourself to "feel the fear and do it anyway" by taking a small step towards facing that fear and embracing the joy and excitement of new experiences.

49

Energy

> *We are always at choice with where we expend our*
> *thought, feeling and action energy. It is when we*
> *channel that energy towards our desired outcomes*
> *that we start to build the life we seek.*

We are always in control of where we expend our thought, feeling, and action energy. The choices we make in how we think, feel, and act ultimately shape the direction of our lives.

When we channel that energy towards our desired outcomes, we start to build the life we seek.

It is easy to get caught up in day-to-day distractions and let our thoughts, feelings, and actions be controlled by external factors. We may find ourselves reacting to the stressors and demands of our environment rather than proactively choosing how to respond.

However, by taking ownership of our thoughts, feelings, and actions, we can start to steer our lives towards our desired outcomes.

For example, if our desired outcome is to lead a more healthy lifestyle, we can channel our thought energy towards positive self-talk and visualisation of our goals.

We can channel our emotional (feeling) energy towards imagining what it would feel like to live in a healthy body, coupled with feelings of motivation and determination and then finally, we can channel our action-oriented energy towards making healthy choices and taking consistent, aligned actions towards our goals.

Journal Prompt: Reflect on how you are currently expending your thought, feeling, and action energy, and explore how you can intentionally channel that energy towards your desired outcomes and start building the life you seek.

50

Patience

Sometimes we have to do the thing we don't want to. We might be bored, or we might feel ill, or we might get frustrated with the time it takes to see any results. Stick with it! Transformation might take time. The amount of time is unknown so we just have to stick with the plan. To ease the monotony keep a record of results to chart progress. When we see small incremental improvements it helps us stay the course.

There are times in life when we are faced with tasks or responsibilities that we don't necessarily want to do. We might be bored with the task at hand, or we might feel ill and not up to the task, or we might get frustrated with the time it takes to see any results. These are all natural reactions and can be tough to overcome, but it's important to remember that transformation can take time.

When we set out to achieve a goal, we often want immediate results. However, transformation can often take time to materialise, so it's important to stick with the plan, even when it feels difficult or monotonous.

One way to ease the monotony is to keep a record of our results. Charting progress can help us see small incremental improvements, which can help us stay the course. These smaller incremental changes build momentum and positive feelings towards the larger transformation.

It's also important to remember that the amount of time it takes to see results is unknown. We can't predict exactly when we'll reach our goal, but by sticking with the plan, we'll get there eventually. It's important to stay focused on the end goal and not get discouraged by the time it takes to achieve it. Use the incremental results and small wins along the journey and celebrate them all.

> **Action step**: Keep a record of your progress, celebrate small wins, and stay focused on your end goal, even when the process feels difficult or monotonous, to maintain momentum towards your desired transformation.

51

Lessons

> *We are here to learn from experience. In some, this may be a recurring aspect of life. Our experiences teach us and help us grow into better versions of ourselves. The experiences are always for us at some level, the experiences never happen to us.*

Experience is one of the most important aspects of life that shape and mould us into who we are today. It is through our experiences that we learn, grow and develop as individuals.

Experiences teach us valuable lessons and provide us with a deeper understanding of the world around us. Whether it is through success or failure, joy or sorrow, our experiences shape us and help us become better versions of ourselves.

One of the key things to remember about experiences is that they are never happening to us but for us. Every experience, good or bad, has a purpose and provides a lesson to be learned. Experiences are a reflection of our predominant focus of attention and emotional response.

It may take time and reflection, but it is important to understand that every experience serves a greater purpose in our personal growth and development. The challenges and obstacles we face in life are opportunities for us to learn and grow, and it is up to us to take advantage of these opportunities and consider changing our perspective or focus.

In some cases, certain experiences may be a recurring aspect of life. This can be frustrating, but it is also a sign that we have not yet fully learned the lesson that experience is trying to teach us and also a sign that we continue to think and feel the same thoughts and emotions about a given subject.

Journal prompt: Reflect on a significant experience in your life and consider the lessons and growth it has brought you, recognising that every experience serves a greater purpose in your personal development.

52

Leap

> *Sometimes you can stretch yourself to reach heights that just a few moments earlier seemed impossible. There's a saying, "Leap and you'll grow wings". When the time is right, and you'll know it deep within you, then take that leap!*

The human mind is capable of remarkable things, and one of them is the ability to push beyond our perceived limitations.

Sometimes, we encounter a situation where we feel like giving up, but with a little bit of courage and determination, we can stretch ourselves to reach heights that seemed impossible just a moment earlier. The key to unlocking our potential is taking that leap of faith when the time feels right.

There's a saying that goes, "Leap and you'll grow wings." This quote perfectly captures the idea that when we take a risk and challenge ourselves, we can achieve things that we never thought possible.

It takes courage to face our fears and to step outside of our comfort zone, but when we do, the rewards can be substantial. When we push ourselves we become stronger, more resilient, and more confident in our abilities.

However, it is important to note that taking that leap should only be done when the time is right. It is essential to listen to our instincts and to trust our gut feelings.

We will know deep within us when it is time to make that leap, and when that time comes, we must be ready to seize the opportunity.

> **Action step**: Trust your instincts and be prepared to take a leap of faith when the time feels right, knowing that pushing beyond your perceived limitations can lead to incredible growth and rewards.

53

Shine

> *Understand who you are and stand in your truth. When we mask and hide who we are we create unhealthy stress and anxiety within us that leads us to question our self-worth. Conversely, when we are truly authentic and have the confidence to stand whole-heartedly and unshakable in the truth of who we are, we discover an inner power so strong that we permit others to shine in their truth too.*

Self-awareness and authenticity are essential components of a fulfilling life. Understanding who we really are, our strengths, weaknesses, values, and beliefs, helps us to live our lives with purpose and direction.

However, when we mask and hide who we really are, it creates unhealthy stress and anxiety that erodes our self-worth and sense of self. This often stems from a fear of not being accepted or loved for who we truly are, leading us to conform to the expectations of others.

On the other hand, when we are authentic and have the confidence to stand in our truth, we empower ourselves and others.

By being true to ourselves, we attract like-minded people who appreciate and respect us for who we are. This creates a strong foundation for meaningful relationships and a sense of belonging.

Additionally, when we stand in our truth, we are more likely to make decisions that align with our values and purpose, leading to a more fulfilling life.

Standing in our truth also gives us an inner power so strong that we can inspire others to do the same. When we model authenticity and self-acceptance, it encourages others to be true to themselves and to shine in their own truth too.

> **Journal prompt**: Reflect on a moment when you felt truly authentic and self-aware, and explore the impact it had on your sense of self, relationships, and overall fulfilment.

54

Faith

> *Sometimes all you have is trust and faith. In the moments when everything seems lost it is possible to find resilience from a place of deep surrender, trust and faith. When nothing makes sense and the mind cannot fathom the solution(s) then that is the time when your resilience, trust and faith will be rewarded. You will somehow get through the storm!*

Life is unpredictable and often presents us with challenges that can shake our confidence and leave us feeling lost.

In these moments, it can be easy to lose faith and give into despair, but it is during these times that trust and faith become our greatest allies.

When everything seems lost and the mind cannot find a solution, it is possible to find resilience from a place of deep surrender, trust, and faith

By surrendering to the unknown and having faith that everything will work out in the end, we can release the burden of control and allow ourselves to be guided by a higher power.

Trusting in a power greater than ourselves can bring a sense of peace and calm, helping us to weather the storm. When we have faith and trust, we can access a well of inner strength that allows us to endure even the toughest challenges.

Furthermore, having trust and faith can bring unexpected rewards. When we surrender control and trust in the journey, we often find that solutions present themselves in ways that we could never have imagined.

Action step: Practice surrendering control and cultivating trust and faith in the face of uncertainty, knowing that there is a greater power guiding you and that solutions will unfold in their own time.

55

Breathe II

> *Intentional deep breathing can have a dramatic positive effect on lowering and stabilising your nervous system and your blood pressure. Never underestimate the power of breath on the body and mind.*

Breathwork is a simple yet powerful tool that can have a profound impact on our physical, emotional, and mental well-being.

Intentional deep breathing can help to lower and stabilise our nervous system and blood pressure, creating a sense of calm and balance in the body.

When we are under stress, our breathing becomes shallow and rapid, leading to increased heart rate and high blood pressure. This can exacerbate feelings of anxiety and tension.

However, by taking slow, deep breaths, we activate the parasympathetic nervous system, which slows down our heart rate and lowers blood pressure, reducing stress and anxiety.

Intentional deep breathing also has a calming effect on the mind. By focusing on our breath, we can quiet the mind and reduce the constant chatter that contributes to stress and anxiety. It creates a sense of grounding and clarity, allowing us to approach life's challenges with a calm and centred perspective.

Intentional deep breathing is a simple and accessible tool that can be done anytime, anywhere.

> Journal prompt: Reflect on the power of intentional deep breathing and explore how incorporating it into your daily routine can bring a sense of calm, balance, and clarity to your mind, body, and overall well-being. Furthermore, just try it and see how much better you feel.

Patience II

During the course of transformation, it can be easy to feel
frustrated and overwhelmed when things don't go according
to plan.

However, it is important to remember that sometimes, things
might have to wait until later and that's okay. This does not
mean anything good or bad, it just is.

We often put a lot of pressure on ourselves to achieve our
goals and meet our expectations. When things don't happen

as quickly as we would like, it can be disheartening and lead to feelings of failure.

However, it is important to recognise that progress often happens at its own pace and sometimes things just need more allowing

By accepting that some things might have to wait until later, we can reduce the stress and anxiety that comes with the pressure to achieve. This allows us to focus on the present moment and enjoy the journey, rather than just the destination.

Moreover, by being patient and allowing things to unfold in their own time, we can open ourselves up to new possibilities and opportunities that may not have been available if we had been in a rush.

Action step: Practice patience and embrace the idea that some things may need to wait, trusting that the timing will align perfectly with your journey, allowing new possibilities to unfold.

57

Resilience

> *When everything seems to be going wrong and things feel like they couldn't get any worse, the truth is they probably could but somehow you will get through it. When you want to give up, don't. You've got this!*

Life is full of ups and downs, and there will be times when everything seems to be going wrong and things feel like they couldn't get any worse.

It is in these moments that it is easy to feel defeated and want to give up.

However, it is important to remember that the truth is

things probably could get worse, but somehow, you will get through it.

When faced with challenges and difficulties, it can be tempting to give in to feelings of hopelessness and despair. However, it is during these times that our inner strength and resilience are tested and we have the opportunity to grow and learn.

The inner relationship we can nurture with our higher selves will be the greatest source of strength and resilience we can ever have. When we find that source of strength we become unshakeable.

By navigating the tough times, we can develop a sense of inner resilience and fortitude that will serve us well in the future.

Journal prompt: Reflect on a challenging experience you have faced and explore how it has contributed to your inner strength and resilience.

58

Support II

> *It's good to talk. Sometimes all we need is to be heard and that's enough. It is healthy to talk about things that are concerning us. Talking can allow us to hear or see a different perspective to a problem. On other occasions, just the mere act of sharing a problem can help us find relief from that problem.*

It's often said that "it's good to talk", and for good reason.

Sometimes, all we need is to be heard and that can be enough to bring us relief and comfort. Talking about things that concern us can be incredibly therapeutic, allowing us to gain new perspectives and insights into our problems.

In a world where people are often so busy and focused on their own lives, it can be easy to feel isolated and disconnected.

When we open up and share our thoughts and feelings, however, we can find a sense of connection and understanding with others.

By talking about our challenges, we not only give ourselves a chance to work through our problems, but we also offer others the opportunity to offer their support and help.

Moreover, talking about our problems can also help us process our emotions and find solutions to our challenges. By speaking openly and honestly about what is troubling us, we can gain new insights, generate new ideas, and ultimately find ways to move forward.

Furthermore, talking about our challenges can also help to reduce feelings of stress and anxiety and promote overall mental wellness.

Action step: Reach out to a trusted friend, family member, or therapist and engage in a meaningful conversation about something that is troubling you.

59

Intention

Sometimes just do what you can. It doesn't have to be grand or make a big statement. Just make it intentional as that is enough.

In our fast-paced and ever-changing world, it can be easy to get overwhelmed by all the things we need to do and the expectations that are placed upon us.

When this happens, it's important to remember that sometimes all we can do is what we can do, and that's okay.

Doing what we can doesn't have to be grand or make a big statement. It just has to be intentional.

By focusing on the things we can control, we can find a sense of peace and satisfaction in our daily lives. When we make our actions intentional, we become more mindful and present in each moment, which can help to reduce stress and anxiety.

Intentional actions can be as simple as taking a few deep breaths, smiling at someone, or making a cup of tea with care and attention.

These small acts of kindness and care can have a positive impact not only on ourselves but also on those around us. They can bring a sense of meaning and purpose to our lives, even on the most challenging of days.

> Journal prompt: Reflect on the small, intentional action you chose to incorporate into your day today and explore how it made you feel and the impact it had on yourself and others.

60

Now

Grab each opportunity to live whenever the moment arises. Live for 'now' and don't wait for circumstances to change.

Life is full of opportunities to live and experience new things, but it can be easy to get caught up in our daily routines and neglect the present moment.

We often put off living until our circumstances change or until we have more time, money, or resources. But the truth is that life is happening right now, and we don't know how much time we have left.

That's why it's important to grab each opportunity to live

whenever the moment arises. We should live for 'now' and not wait for circumstances to change.

This means taking the time to enjoy the small things in life, like a beautiful sunset or a good cup of coffee.

It means being present in the moment and savouring the experience, whether it's spending time with loved ones or taking a walk in nature.

Living for 'now' also means taking risks and trying new things, even if they may be outside our comfort zone. When we step out of our comfort zone, we grow and learn more about ourselves and the world around us.

> **Action step**: Take a moment today to consciously embrace the present moment and seize an opportunity to try something new, whether it's a new activity, a new perspective, or a new experience, and fully immerse yourself in the richness of the present.

61

Love II

Love is the light that will illuminate the way in the darkest of seasons.

Love is a powerful and transformative force that has the ability to bring light to even the darkest of seasons.

Whether we are facing difficult personal struggles, global challenges, or simply feeling lost and alone, love has the power to guide us and give us hope.

Love has a unique way of illuminating the path ahead and showing us the way, even when everything else seems uncertain. It is a light that shines bright and strong, offering comfort, support, and guidance to those in need.

Love also has the ability to bring people together, inspiring us to work together and help one another through even the toughest of times.

In our darkest moments, love can provide the comfort and support we need to get through. Whether it's the love of a partner, family, friends, or even a stranger, it is a powerful force that has the ability to change our lives.

But love is not just associated with our relationship with others; love is the love for ourselves that we feel deep in our hearts. Self-love is about being kind to oneself and being able to quiet the inner critic through feelings of self-compassion and self-forgiveness. This inner love is probably the most powerful love of all.

Journal prompt: Reflect on the power of love and its transformative nature in your life, and explore how you can cultivate and share love in your relationships, community, and most importantly, within yourself.

62

Miracles

Miracles do happen. The best thing you can do is just get out of the way to let the universe do its thing.

Miracles are real, and they happen all around us every day.

While they may seem rare or impossible to some, they are a testament to the power of the universe and the infinite possibilities that exist within it.

One of the best things we can do to experience miracles is to simply get out of the way. When we surrender control and allow the universe to take the reins, we open ourselves up to a world of infinite possibilities and allow the universe to work its magic.

The universe has a way of orchestrating events and bringing people together in unexpected and miraculous ways. By trusting in the process and letting go of our control, we can tap into this infinite power and experience the magic of the universe firsthand.

To experience miracles we have to be open to them. When we approach life with an open mind and a positive outlook, we become more receptive to the unexpected and the miraculous. We allow the universe to work its magic, and we become more open to the possibility of experiencing something truly amazing.

> **Action step**: Take a moment today to surrender control, trust in the process, and be open to the possibility of miracles unfolding in your life, allowing the universe to work its magic.

63

Love III

> *Love is the guiding light that can hold everything together.*

Love is the most powerful force in the universe, and it has the power to bring people together, heal wounds, and guide us through the darkest of times.

When we open our hearts to love, we become more connected to ourselves, the world around us and to the people in our lives.

Love is a guiding light that shines through the darkness and helps us to find our way. It provides us with a sense of direction and purpose, and it helps us to navigate the challenges and obstacles that we face in life.

Whether we are dealing with personal struggles or facing the challenges of the world around us, love provides us with the strength and resilience that we need to keep going.

Love is also the glue that holds everything together. It provides us with a sense of security and stability, and it helps us to build relationships that last. When we love and are loved in return, we create a sense of belonging and community that helps us to thrive.

The most powerful of all love is the love for yourself. Tap into the power of love in your own heart. Having a loving relationship with your inner self provides peace in difficult times. Inner love is the fuel that helps us become more resilient and able to navigate life's challenges.

Journal prompt: Reflect on the power of love in your life and how it has guided you through challenging times, and explore ways to cultivate and nurture love within yourself and your relationships in your journal today.

64

Action

> *Sometimes making the effort to do something can make a difference and can re-energise you; try it!*

Making the effort to do something, no matter how small, can have a significant impact on our energy levels and overall well-being.

When we are feeling down or stuck, it can be easy to get caught up in negative thoughts and feelings, causing us to spiral into a state of stagnation.

However, making the effort to do something, even if it's just going for a walk or completing a simple task, can help shift our energy and bring a new perspective to our lives.

Taking action can be a powerful motivator, helping us to break through the barriers that are holding us back.

By making the effort to do something, we give ourselves the opportunity to see that we are capable of making positive changes, and this can help us to build momentum and move forward.

Furthermore, the sense of accomplishment that comes from completing a task can boost our self-esteem and improve our overall mood.

Action steps: Take a moment to identify one small action you can take today to uplift your energy and well-being and commit to making the effort to do it with intention and positivity.

65

Laugh

> *Humour is fantastic medicine, alleviating mental, emotional and physical dis-ease. Try to find something to lift the mood a little and laugh. Maybe a funny film or podcast might help. Suffering can ease with laughter.*

Humour has the power to lighten up even the toughest of situations and bring a smile to our faces.

It has the ability to ease our mental, emotional, and physical diseases, making us feel better and happier.

Whether it's watching a funny movie, listening to a hilarious podcast, or simply finding something to joke about, incorporating humour into our lives can greatly improve our well-being.

Laughter has been shown to release endorphins, which are natural painkillers, and reduce levels of stress hormones such as cortisol and adrenaline.

These effects help to reduce feelings of anxiety and depression and can even improve physical health by boosting the immune system and reducing inflammation.

In addition, humour can also bring people together and foster a sense of community. Sharing a good laugh with friends or family can help us to connect and bond on a deeper level, which is essential for our overall happiness and well-being.

If you're feeling overwhelmed or stressed, try to find something that brings a smile to your face. You might just be surprised by how much better you'll feel.

> **Journal prompt**: Reflect on a funny or lighthearted moment that has brought joy to your life, and write about the impact it had on your overall well-being and perspective.

66

Surrender

> *Even though your ego-mind might be screaming at you and filling you with worry and fear, there will come a point where the only thing to do is surrender. That doesn't mean quitting. It means surrender to the unknown. Surrender control of having everything worked out. Sometimes you have to trust and believe that the universe has your back!*

Surrendering to the unknown can be a difficult concept for many people, as it involves letting go of control and trusting in a higher power.

The ego-mind often creates worry and fear in an effort to control the situation, but this only leads to further stress and anxiety. Instead, surrendering to the unknown can bring a sense of peace and calmness to the mind and body.

Surrendering does not mean quitting or giving up, but rather it means accepting that the outcome may not always be in our control.

It is about trusting the universe and having faith that everything will work out in the end.

This can be a liberating experience, as it takes the pressure off and allows us to focus on the present moment.

When we surrender in this way, we are able to release the worries and fears that are holding us back and instead embrace the journey, even if it is uncertain. This can lead to a more fulfilling life as we are no longer burdened by the weight of control and instead can live freely in the moment.

Surrendering control in this way can also create space in the mind for clarity which then allows for an increased flow in creativity.

Action step: Take a moment to reflect on an area of your life where you feel the need to have control and consider one step you can take to surrender that control and trust in the flow of the universe.

67

Self-Compassion

> *Be kind to yourself. By finding a space of peace and quiet, we can also find an ability to be kind to ourselves to allow a deeper healing to occur. It is not uncommon to find ourselves in totally unplanned and unforeseen circumstances that can cause a significant stress response in our bodies.*

Self-compassion is a critical aspect of our mental and emotional well-being.

In the midst of chaos and uncertainty, it is easy to get caught up in feelings of stress, anxiety, and self-doubt. However, it is important to remember to take a step back and be kind to ourselves.

This can be achieved by finding moments of peace and quiet where we can reflect on our thoughts and feelings and offer ourselves compassion and understanding.

When we practice self-compassion, we can allow our bodies to enter a state of relaxation and promote a deeper healing process.

Self-compassion helps us to shift our focus from self-criticism to self-care. By being gentle and understanding with ourselves, we can foster a positive relationship with our bodies and minds, leading to increased resilience and improved overall well-being.

So taking the time to be kind to yourself, particularly in difficult and challenging circumstances, can have a profound impact on your mental and emotional health. By prioritising self-compassion, it's possible to find peace, healing, and a renewed sense of strength to tackle life's obstacles.

Journal prompt: Reflect on a recent challenging situation or personal struggle and explore how you can practice self-compassion and offer yourself kindness and understanding in the midst of it.

68

Release

It's good to cry. Holding onto emotional pain and trauma can be extremely unhealthy. Emotions like anger, sadness, hurt and bitterness can cause dis-ease in the body. Although difficult to face, the free-dom that can be experienced from the release of emotional pain is euphoric.

It used to be said that crying is a sign of weakness, but in reality, it is a powerful and cathartic release.

Holding onto emotional pain and trauma is not only un-healthy, it can lead to dis-ease in the body and mind. Negative emotions like anger, sadness, hurt, and bitterness can cause a significant amount of stress and tension in our lives.

When we let ourselves cry and truly feel these emotions, we allow them to be released and processed, rather than bottling them up inside. This can lead to a profound sense of peace and liberation.

Crying is a natural and healthy way to deal with difficult emotions and it should not be stigmatised or suppressed. It allows us to let go of the past, heal from our wounds, and move forward with a renewed sense of hope and strength.

By giving ourselves permission to cry, we can begin the process of emotional healing and find peace within ourselves.

So, the next time you feel the urge to cry, embrace it and let it wash over you. You will be surprised at how much better you feel afterwards.

Action Step: Give yourself permission to cry and release any pent-up emotions you may be holding onto, allowing yourself to heal and find peace within.

69

Knowing

> *There may come a point when God/the Universe/*
> *Divine Intelligence/Source Energy speaks to your*
> *heart. Let that knowing soothe your tired heart, let*
> *that knowing replenish your body. Let that knowing*
> *be your power and your fuel. It is unlikely that you*
> *will hear this audibly, it will come in the form of a*
> *deep sense of knowing in your body (your diminished*
> *soul is re-ignited).*

It is often said that when we truly listen to our hearts, we can hear the voice of a higher power guiding us towards our purpose in life or lifting us in times of need.

This feeling of inner peace and contentment can provide us

with the strength and resilience we need to navigate through the challenges of life. The connection to a higher power can bring us a sense of comfort and security, knowing that we are not alone in our journey.

This deep sense of knowing can provide us with the courage to make difficult decisions and trust that everything will work out for the best in the end. Even when everything around us is showing us evidence that is contrary to that outcome. The knowledge that we are supported and guided by a higher power can help us to release our fears and worries, allowing us to focus on the present moment.

This connection can provide us with the energy and motivation we need to keep moving forward, even in the face of extreme adversity.

By embracing this sense of inner peace and trusting in the guidance of the universe, we can find the strength to overcome any obstacle and live a life of joy and fulfilment.

> Journal prompt: Take a moment to listen to the voice of your heart and reflect on the guidance and support you receive from a higher power, and how it can empower you to navigate through life's challenges with strength and resilience.

70

Challenge

> *The brain needs to be tested and pushed to make new neurological pathways and new neurology is the basis of all transformation. Playing safe will always keep you where you are right now. Find ways to test yourself and repeat those exercises to strengthen the new neurology.*

The human brain is a remarkable and complex organ that has the ability to adapt, change and grow. This process is known as neuroplasticity and it is a vital aspect of our development and learning.

However, for new neurological pathways to be formed, it is essential that the brain is pushed and challenged. This can be achieved through learning new skills, trying new activities and engaging in different forms of mental stimulation. By playing it safe and sticking to familiar routines, we limit our ability to form new neurological pathways and make positive changes in our lives.

It's important to find ways to challenge ourselves and to push beyond our comfort zones, whether that's learning a new language, taking up a new hobby, or engaging in a physical activity. The more we push ourselves, the stronger the new neurological pathways become, and the more we can develop and grow as individuals.

Moreover, the repetition of these exercises is key to strengthening the new neurology. By regularly testing and challenging our brains, we can continue to build new pathways and make real and lasting changes in our lives.

To transform your life and make positive changes, it's essential to push yourself out of your comfort zone and engage in activities that challenge and stimulate your brain.

Action step: Take a step outside your comfort zone today and engage in an activity or learn something new that challenges and stimulates your brain, promoting neuroplasticity and personal growth.

71

Faith II

Having true faith is having blind faith. There will be many who will oppose your faith by attempting to aggravate fears and doubts within you. They will question you for evidence or proof which you cannot produce. If there was evidence and proof there would be no need for faith. That is the point of faith.

Faith is a powerful force that can guide us through life's challenges and bring us comfort in difficult times.

True faith, however, requires a willingness to let go of rational thinking and embrace a sense of belief that cannot be proven or quantified.

When we have faith, we trust in something greater than ourselves, even when there is no tangible evidence to support it. This kind of faith is often referred to as "blind faith" because it asks us to trust in the unknown and the unseen.

Despite this, it is not uncommon for others to try and challenge our faith by questioning our beliefs or trying to sow the seeds of doubt.

However, it is important to remember that faith is a personal journey and cannot be fully understood or appreciated by others. The true test of faith is not in the evidence or proof we can provide, but in the way we live our lives and the peace and comfort it brings us.

Having true faith means being willing to take that leap of faith and trust in the power of something greater than ourselves. It is a journey of self-discovery and personal growth, where we find comfort in the knowledge that we are never alone and that there is a higher power guiding us on our path.

Journal prompt: Reflect on the role of faith in your life and how it guides you through challenges and brings you comfort, even in the absence of tangible evidence or proof.

72

Possibilities II

The world is a playground of possibilities. Those possibilities can manifest in our experience through creative thought and feelings accompanied by aligned actions. This is like a seismic shift in conscious awareness and creation.

It is a fact that we live in a world of limitless possibilities. However, it is not always easy to tap into these possibilities and bring them into our lives.

This is where the power of creative thought and aligned action comes into play.

Our thoughts and feelings are incredibly powerful, and when

we focus them in a specific direction, they can manifest into physical reality. This is a profound shift in conscious awareness, where we become the creators of our own reality.

The key is to focus on positive thoughts and feelings and to align our actions with these thoughts and feelings. This is where true manifestation begins. When we do this, we can create an environment where anything is possible, and where our dreams and desires can become a reality.

The world is truly a playground of possibilities, but it is up to us to choose which possibilities we bring into our lives.

If we focus on positivity, love, and compassion, then the possibilities that come into our experience will be of a similar nature. On the other hand, if we focus on fear, anger, and negativity, then that is what we will attract into our lives.

> **Action step**: Take a moment to reflect on your thoughts, feelings, and actions, and consider how they align with the possibilities you want to bring into your life. Take aligned action towards your desires and consciously choose positive thoughts and feelings to manifest the reality you desire.

73

Love IV

When you are ready, your heart will begin to fill with love for yourself. This is a beautiful feeling and one to be cherished.

Self-love is a crucial aspect of one's overall well-being and happiness.

When we are able to love ourselves, we can radiate positivity and attract more love and positivity into our lives.

The process of self-love may be challenging, as it requires us to look within and acknowledge both our strengths and weaknesses. However, when we are ready and open to it, the journey can be incredibly rewarding.

As we learn to love ourselves, we can let go of past hurt and embrace the present moment with an open heart. We become more accepting of who we are and are able to recognise our worth. This self-acceptance and self-appreciation allows us to let go of negative self-talk and focus on the positive aspects of ourselves.

Having love for ourselves allows us to set healthy boundaries and prioritise our well-being. We become more confident and are able to assert ourselves in situations that previously caused us stress or anxiety.

Ultimately, self-love paves the way for a more fulfilling life, as we are able to attract positive relationships and experiences into our lives.

> **Journal prompt:** Reflect on one thing you can do to-day to show yourself love and kindness, whether it's practicing self-care, setting boundaries, or affirming your worth.

74

Becoming

Be-Do-Have is one of the secrets to transformation. We must be the person we want to become and take the aligned action to have the rewards or benefits associated with that becoming.

The concept of "Be-Do-Have" is a powerful tool for personal transformation and growth.

It starts with the idea that our actions and behaviours are driven by the person we believe ourselves to be. If we want to change our circumstances and achieve different outcomes, we need to transform the person we see ourselves as being.

This is where "Be" comes in. We must first identify the

qualities and characteristics of the person we want to become and then embody them in our thoughts, feelings, and actions.

Once we have embraced this new identity, it is time to "Do". We must take aligned actions that are in line with the person we want to be. These actions will reinforce our new identity and help us move closer to our desired outcomes.

Finally, the "Have" aspect refers to the rewards and benefits that come with our transformation.

When we have become the person we want to be and taken the appropriate actions, we will naturally begin to experience the fruits of our labour. Our experiences, relationships, and circumstances will change as a result of our transformation.

> **Action step**: Take a moment to reflect on the person you want to become and identify one feeling you can have that aligns with that vision. Start to feel your way to your vision.

75

Happiness

> *Do what makes you happy. Being in your happy flow*
> *state will benefit your entire well-being. If you love a*
> *hobby or pastime, do more of that. Those who can*
> *find a state of flow are often truly happy in their work*
> *and feel like they're not doing work at all.*

Finding happiness is an important aspect of life.

It not only benefits our mental and emotional well-being, but it also has physical health benefits. When we engage in activities that bring us joy, we enter into a state of flow where time seems to stand still and we become fully immersed in the present moment. This flow state can lead to increased creativity, higher levels of productivity, and a greater sense of satisfaction in life.

However, often we get caught up in the demands of daily life and forget to prioritise our own happiness.

We may even push aside our interests and hobbies in favour of more "practical" pursuits. But it is crucial to remember that our happiness should be a top priority.

When we engage in activities that bring us joy, our bodies release endorphins which boost our mood and lower levels of stress and anxiety.

So, do what makes you happy. If you have a passion for photography, take more pictures. If you enjoy cooking, try new recipes and experiment in the kitchen. If you love hiking, go for more walks in nature.

> Journal prompt: Reflect on the activities or hobbies that bring you joy and make a list of three things you can do this week to prioritise your happiness.

76

Nature IV

> *Go to places that inspire you. When you're in those places (such as woodland or on the beach), notice the natural beauty all around you and use that beauty as a source of inspiration. Remember to make notes of the ideas and thoughts that come to you.*

Going to inspiring places can have a profound impact on our creativity and well-being.

Being surrounded by nature, or places that evoke a sense of peace and awe, can open our minds and hearts to new ideas and perspectives. It can also help us to connect with our inner selves and find a sense of balance.

When we allow ourselves to fully immerse in these environments, we can tap into a deep well of inspiration that can fuel our passions and aspirations.

Taking the time to be in these inspiring places can also boost our mood and reduce stress levels.

Being exposed to nature has a calming effect on the body and can even improve physical health. Whether it be taking a walk in a park, sitting by a lake or ocean, or simply admiring a sunset, connecting with nature can refresh and revitalise us; it's good for the soul.

By making a conscious effort to seek out inspiring places and allowing ourselves to be in the moment, we can reap the many benefits that come with being in these environments. So why not try to find some inspiring places near you and allow yourself to be inspired, rejuvenated and re-energised?

Action step: Recharge your creativity and well-being by immersing yourself in inspiring places. Seek out nature's embrace - parks, lakes, or scenic spots - and let the calming surroundings fuel your inspiration and rejuvenate your spirit.

77

Awareness

> *"You are what you think." Instead of allowing your thoughts to run on autopilot try to consciously choose your thoughts to match the new reality that you are building for yourself. This is not as easy as it sounds but with practice your awareness will become more tuned to detecting the presence of the autopilot and you can consciously choose a better thought.*

"You are what you think" is a powerful statement that highlights the impact of our thoughts on our lives.

Our thoughts can shape our experiences, perceptions, and ultimately, our reality. It's crucial that we become more mindful of our thoughts and start to make a conscious effort to choose them carefully.

The process of intentionally choosing our thoughts can help us create a new reality for ourselves, one that is more positive, empowering, and fulfilling. The first step in this process is to increase our awareness of our thoughts.

Often, our thoughts run on autopilot, and we're not even aware of what we're thinking.

By paying close attention to our thoughts, we can start to identify patterns and negative thought processes that are holding us back.

Once we become more aware of our thoughts, we can start to choose them more deliberately. This means intentionally selecting thoughts that align with the reality we want to create for ourselves.

It may be difficult at first, but with practice, it becomes easier to catch our thoughts and redirect them to more positive and empowering ones.

Journal Prompt: Reflect on the power of your thoughts. Take a moment to become aware of your current thought patterns and consider how consciously choosing empowering thoughts can shape a more positive and fulfilling reality for yourself.

78

Relax II

> *Sometimes it's easier to move with the tide and join in rather than resist. Continual resistance can lead to a greater level of frustration, bitterness or anger which is not great.*

Going against the tide and resisting can be draining and can take a toll on one's mental and emotional health.

On the other hand, moving with the tide and finding ways to work with the flow can help reduce stress and promote a sense of peace and well-being.

Instead of fighting against the current, we can learn to navigate and harness its power, making the journey much easier and less tumultuous.

Joining in and working with the flow doesn't mean giving up one's values or beliefs, or people pleasing, but rather finding a way to balance one's own beliefs and values with the reality of the situation.

For example, if there is a change in the workplace that one doesn't agree with, instead of resisting and causing conflict, one can look for ways to work within the change and make the best of the situation.

By being open and flexible, we can find new opportunities and perspectives that may not have been visible before.

We can also learn to be more adaptable and resilient, which will serve us well in the long run.

> **Action Step**: Reflect on a situation in your life where you have been resisting or going against the flow. Consider how you can shift your approach and find ways to work with the current instead, aligning your values and beliefs while seeking opportunities for growth and harmony. Take one small step today to embrace the flow and observe the positive impact it has on your mental and emotional well-being.

79

Strength

> *When it feels like God's plan is pushing you to break-*
> *ing point, hang on in there and resist the temptation*
> *to let fear dominate your thinking. Try to see and feel*
> *the love and beauty in everything. It might be hard*
> *but it is there. When you feel that love you can also*
> *imagine a brighter future.*

In tough moments, it's tempting to yield to fear and anxiety, but it's crucial to recognize that even amid the greatest challenges, love and beauty persist in the world.

Anchoring yourself to this sense of hope and positivity can provide grounding and motivation, especially when it feels like you're on the verge of breaking.

To navigate these times, resist the pull of fear dominating your thoughts. Instead, deliberately redirect your focus to finding love and beauty in everything, no matter how small. Whether it's taking a moment to revel in the beauty of nature or expressing gratitude for the people and experiences in your life, these small acts can be powerful.

Visualising a future filled with love, joy, and alignment with your plans can bring comfort and inspiration during difficult periods. Envisioning this positive future fosters hope, even when it seems like the universe is testing your limits.

Ultimately, the key to mental strength and resilience lies in having faith and trust in the enduring presence of love and beauty, even in the darkest moments.

By intentionally shifting your focus away from fear and anxiety, lifting your mood becomes possible, allowing the inherent love within you to expand and influence your perspective.

> **Journal Prompt**: Take a moment to reflect on a challenging situation you're currently facing. How can you shift your focus from fear and anxiety to love and beauty? Write down three things you appreciate and find beautiful in your life right now, no matter how small they may seem. Consider how embracing this perspective can bring you comfort and support during difficult times.

80

Love V

> *Through the power of universal love, it is possible to imagine whatever life we want for ourselves. We can imagine and feel that future in the heart, and then hold our patience with continuing trust and belief.*

The power of love is a transformative force that can be harnessed to shape our lives in profound ways.

It provides us with the ability to imagine and envision a future that is rich with possibility and fulfilment.

When we tap into the power of universal love, we can let our hearts soar, imagining the life that we truly want for ourselves.

This kind of visualisation can help us to anchor our faith and belief in a brighter future, even when the present moment feels uncertain or challenging.

By taking the time to focus on the love that is within us and surrounds us, we can feel our spirits lift, and begin to see the world in a new light. It's important to remember that love starts within and we don't become dependent upon an external love.

Through the power of that inner love, we can begin to dream bigger, to imagine a life that is rich with purpose, joy, and fulfilment. And as we hold fast to that vision, we can feel the power of love guiding us towards a brighter, more beautiful future.

Action Step: Set aside dedicated time each day to connect with the power of love within yourself. Close your eyes, take deep breaths, and visualise the life you desire, infused with feelings of love and fulfilment. Allow this vision to inspire and guide your actions towards creating a future aligned with the power of love.

81

Glory

> *When you find that sense of knowing you know that*
> *your transformation is starting to unfold for you.*
> *Bask in this glorious feeling.*

Transformation can be a difficult and challenging process, but when you finally find that sense of knowing, it is a truly joyful moment.

The feeling of knowing that you are on the right path and that your life is starting to unfold in the way you want is indescribable.

It is a moment that fills you with hope, excitement, and peace.

This moment marks the beginning of your journey towards your true self and the manifestation of your deepest desires.

As you bask in this glorious feeling, take a moment to appreciate the journey that has led you to this point. Take stock of the lessons you have learned, the challenges you have faced, and the growth you have experienced.

Remember that every step of your journey has been necessary to bring you to this moment of knowing. Now, it's time to embrace your newfound sense of clarity and trust that the universe has your back. Hold onto that knowing and let it guide you forward.

Know that you are capable of creating the life you want and that anything is possible when you have faith in yourself and the universe.

Journal Prompt: Reflect on a moment in your life when you experienced a deep sense of knowing and clarity about your path and purpose. How did it feel? What lessons did you learn along the way? How can you carry that sense of knowing forward in your current journey?

82

Emergence

> *Embrace the new you as 'you' emerge. Aspects of your character may have changed or been enhanced as you transform. This is normal and to be expected. This IS the point of transformation.*

Transformation is a journey of self-discovery and growth.

As we navigate through life, we encounter challenges and experiences that shape and mould us into the person we are meant to be. The process of transformation can be both exhilarating and scary, but it is important to embrace the new you as you emerge.

During this process, aspects of your character may have

changed or been enhanced. This is normal and to be expected. The point of transformation is to become the best version of yourself, and as such, it is important to embrace these changes with open arms.

The changes may be subtle or they may be drastic, but either way, they are a testament to the growth and development you have undergone.

It is also important to remember that transformation is not a one-time event. It is a continuous process, and as such, you must be willing to continue learning, growing, and adapting to the new you.

This journey is not always easy, but it is worth it.

Embrace the new you, and allow yourself to be transformed into the person you were always meant to be.

Action Step: Embrace the process of transformation and continue to nurture your personal growth by embracing change, learning, and adapting to the new version of yourself.

83

Ideas

> *When the ideas start to flow, find a way to capture them in a way that works for you. Some people keep a pen and paper close by, others might use their smartphone to capture notes or record voice notes. It doesn't matter what medium you prefer, but capture the ideas, because when they flow, they will flow fast!*

Capturing ideas is an important aspect of transformation.

When the creative energy is flowing, we can be overflowing with ideas, thoughts, and insights. If we don't have a way to capture these thoughts, they can easily be forgotten, lost, or distorted. Having a system in place to capture these ideas can help us stay organised and focused on our goals and aspirations.

Some people prefer traditional methods such as pen and paper, and a journal, while others prefer digital tools such as voice notes or note-taking apps.

Whatever medium works best for you, it's important to have it readily available so you can capture those ideas when they come.

The beauty of capturing ideas is that they can be referred back to later when you need inspiration or motivation. They can also be expanded upon and turned into actionable steps that bring us closer to realising our goals and aspirations.

Capturing ideas is an essential step in the transformation process. By finding a way that works for you, you can preserve the creative energy that flows through you and use it to bring positive change and growth into your life.

> **Journal Prompt:** Reflect on your preferred method of capturing ideas and explore how it has helped you in your personal transformation journey, allowing you to harness and build upon the creative energy that flows within you.

84

Acceptance II

> *Love who you are and embrace your characteristics.*
> *The greater resistance you build up about yourself,*
> *the more that unwanted behaviour will reveal itself.*
> *Relax and love all of who you are.*

Loving and accepting oneself is an essential aspect of living a fulfilling life.

It is easy to get caught up in the expectations of others or the pressure to conform to societal standards, but in doing so, we risk losing sight of our true selves. Embracing our unique characteristics and quirks is a powerful way to build self-confidence and cultivate a positive self-image.

When we resist aspects of ourselves, whether it be physical attributes or personality traits, we create an internal conflict that can manifest as negative behaviours or thought patterns.

However, by accepting and celebrating our individuality, we can learn to appreciate ourselves more fully and create a positive relationship with our self-image.

It's important to remember that everyone is perfect just as they are. Even our flaws and imperfections make us unique and interesting. When we learn to love ourselves and all of our quirks, we become more authentic and confident in our interactions with others.

The key to building a positive self-image and cultivating self-love is to embrace all of our characteristics. By letting go of our resistance to ourselves, we can unlock our true potential and live a more fulfilling life.

> **Action Step:** Take a moment each day to consciously embrace and celebrate your unique qualities and quirks, allowing self-acceptance to guide you towards a more fulfilling and confident life.

85

Courage

Do the things that you might think scare you. When you face your fears and do the things that you think might trigger you, you might be surprised that the situation will be fine and any fear will immediately dissipate.

It's natural to feel apprehensive or scared about new experiences or challenges.

However, by facing our fears and doing the things that we think might scare us, we can build resilience and confidence. Often, our fears stem from the unknown, and we imagine the worst-case scenario. In reality, the situation is usually not as bad as we anticipated.

By stepping out of our comfort zones, we can push ourselves to grow and expand our horizons. When we face our fears and overcome challenges, we learn valuable lessons about ourselves and our capabilities. We may discover hidden strengths and abilities that we never knew we had.

It's important to remember that fear is a natural human emotion and can be a healthy response to certain situations.

However, when we allow fear to hold us back from pursuing our goals and dreams, we limit our potential and miss out on valuable opportunities.

Facing our fears and doing the things that we think might scare us is an important part of personal growth and development. We develop courage and that is the ability to act in spite of our fears.

Journal Prompt: Reflect on a time when you faced a fear or tackled a challenge, and explore how it helped you grow and discover new strengths within yourself.

86

Thoughts IV

All transformation starts in the imagination with thoughts and ideas. All thoughts expand the spiritual universe so try hard to become aware of your thoughts. Think thoughts of love to expand the universe in a loving way.

Our thoughts and imagination have a powerful influence on the course of our lives.

The things we think about and focus on have the potential to transform our world and the universe as a whole. It is through our imagination and thoughts that we can create new possibilities and transform our reality.

When we allow ourselves to dream and imagine, we open up new pathways for growth and transformation. Our thoughts can take us beyond our current circumstances and limitations, and enable us to envision a brighter future.

However, not all thoughts are created equal. Our thoughts have the power to either uplift us or bring us down.

Negative and self-defeating thoughts can limit our potential and prevent us from achieving our goals, while positive and loving thoughts can expand our spiritual universe and bring us closer to our dreams.

To harness the power of our thoughts for positive transformation, we must become aware of our thinking patterns and consciously choose to focus on thoughts of love, abundance, and possibility. By doing so, we can expand the spiritual universe in a loving way and manifest our deepest desires.

> **Action Step**: Take a few moments each day to consciously choose and cultivate positive and empowering thoughts, envisioning the life you desire and embracing the power of your imagination to create positive transformations in your reality.

87

Gifts

Sometimes the universe can move us and deliver to us things that we could never plan ourselves and all we have to do is be willing to graciously receive with thankful hearts.

The universe has a way of working in mysterious ways and often delivers unexpected gifts and blessings that we could never have planned for ourselves.

Whether it's a chance encounter, a job opportunity, or a new relationship, these experiences can be life-changing and transformative.

To receive these gifts from the universe, we must be willing to let go of our expectations and trust in the natural flow of life. This means being open to new opportunities and experiences, even if they don't fit into our preconceived plans or ideas.

When we approach life with an open and grateful heart, we create space for the universe to work its magic. Instead of struggling and forcing things to happen, we allow things to unfold naturally, and trust that everything is happening for our highest good.

It's important to remember that receiving gifts from the universe is not about luck or chance, but about being in alignment with our true purpose and values.

When we are true to ourselves and live in harmony with our innermost desires, the universe responds by sending us exactly what we need at the right time.

Journal Prompt: Reflect on a time when you received an unexpected gift or blessing from the universe, and explore how it transformed your life and deepened your trust in the natural flow of life.

88

Harmony

It is the combination of masculine and feminine energy working together in harmony that yields incredible results.

The concept of masculine and feminine energy goes far beyond gender and relates to the qualities and characteristics that are traditionally associated with these energies.

Masculine energy is often seen as being assertive, decisive, and focused on achieving goals, while feminine energy is often associated with nurturing, intuition, and creativity. Both energies are present in both genders and moreover, both energies are present everywhere and in all things.

When these energies work together in harmony, they can produce incredible results. Masculine energy provides the drive and direction, while feminine energy adds depth, compassion, and creativity to the mix. By integrating these energies, we can tap into a powerful source of strength and inspiration that can help us achieve our goals and dreams.

In personal relationships, integrating masculine and feminine energies creates balance and harmony.

In the workplace, it fosters collaboration, creativity, and success.

Action Step: Reflect on how you can consciously integrate both masculine and feminine energies within yourself, relationships, and work, to create a harmonious balance that maximises your potential and promotes growth and success.

89

Emotional Intelligence

> *Mastery of Advanced Emotional Intelligence is one of the most powerful tools for self-actualisation and transformation.*

Emotional intelligence is the ability to recognise, understand, and manage our own emotions, as well as the emotions of others.

While basic emotional intelligence is important for personal growth and success, mastery of advanced emotional intelligence can be a powerful tool for self-actualisation and transformation.

Advanced emotional intelligence goes beyond self-awareness

and empathy towards others, and involves a deep understanding of the complex interplay of emotions and how they impact our thoughts, behaviours, and relationships. Additionally, advanced emotional intelligence encompasses the ability to find healing and lessons from former emotional experiences. Furthermore, mastery of advanced emotional intelligence helps us towards the attainment of our desires by understanding the gap between us and our desires through the interpretation of our feelings.

By mastering these skills, we can gain greater control over our thoughts and beliefs, and learn to respond to situations in a more effective and positive way.

Mastery of advanced emotional intelligence can help us to identify and overcome limiting beliefs, negative thought patterns, and self-sabotaging behaviours.

It can also help us to develop greater self-confidence, resilience, and interpersonal skills, leading to more fulfilling relationships and success across all aspects of life.

Journal Prompt: Reflect on your journey of emotional intelligence and consider one area where you would like to develop and master advanced emotional intelligence to enhance your personal growth and transformation.

90

Impact

Every lesson that we learn on our soul path could help someone else; always consider how your lessons could help others.

Our soul path is a journey of personal growth and transformation that leads us towards a deeper understanding of ourselves and our place in the world.

Along this path, we encounter many challenges and obstacles, as well as opportunities for learning and growth.

Every lesson that we learn on our soul path has the potential to help someone else who may be going through a similar experience.

By sharing our experiences and insights, we can offer support, guidance, and encouragement to others who are facing similar challenges.

When we consider how our own lessons could help others, we shift our focus from solely our own personal growth to making a positive impact on the world around us.

By sharing our experiences, we can create a ripple effect of positive change, helping others to navigate their own journeys and find greater meaning and purpose in their lives.

Furthermore, by sharing our lessons with others, we deepen our own understanding and internalise the insights we have gained.

> **Action Step**: Reflect on your soul path journey and identify one lesson or insight that you can share with others to inspire and support their personal growth and transformation.

91

Gratitude IV

Never take anything for granted. Develop a deep sense of gratitude for everything in your world. Not a superficial surface-level appreciation but a gratitude that is an outpouring of love from your heart.

Gratitude is a powerful force that can transform our lives and our relationship with the world around us.

When we develop a deep sense of gratitude, we open ourselves up to a greater sense of joy, peace, and abundance, and can overcome feelings of anxiety, stress, and dissatisfaction.

One of the keys to cultivating gratitude is to never take anything for granted. This means recognising and appreciating the many blessings in our lives, both big and small, and being mindful of the many ways in which we are supported and cared for by the world around us.

When we develop a deep sense of gratitude, it goes beyond a superficial, surface-level appreciation. It becomes an outpouring of love from our hearts.

Gratitude can be practiced in many ways, such as keeping a gratitude journal, taking time each day to reflect on the things we are thankful for, or expressing our gratitude to the people in our lives who have made a difference.

Developing a deep sense of gratitude is essential to living a happy and fulfilling life. By recognising and appreciating the many blessings in our lives, we can cultivate a sense of joy, peace, and abundance, and overcome feelings of anxiety, stress, and dissatisfaction.

Journal Prompt: Take a moment to reflect on the blessings in your life and write down five things you are deeply grateful for, expressing why each one holds meaning to you.

92

The Unknown

> *If your life has been literally "turned upside-down", it can become the catalyst and opportunity to become more than you ever previously imagined.*

Life is full of unexpected twists and turns, and sometimes we find ourselves in situations where our lives are turned upside down. In my case, the effects of the stroke literally turned my world upside down (well by 90 degrees at least!) and then metaphorically too as I had to reboot my entire existence as a human being.

This can be a difficult and disorienting experience, but it can also be an opportunity for growth and transformation.

When our lives are turned upside down, it can be a catalyst for change, forcing us to confront our deepest fears and insecurities and reevaluate our priorities and values. This can be a challenging and sometimes painful process, but it can also be a powerful opportunity to become more than we ever imagined.

Through the process of facing our fears and embracing the unknown, we can develop greater resilience, courage, and inner strength. We can learn to trust in ourselves and our abilities and to tap into our deepest potential.

In order to make the most of this opportunity, it is important to approach the situation with an open mind and heart and to be willing to embrace the unknown. By embracing the unknown, facing our fears, and developing greater resilience and inner strength, we can become more than we ever imagined.

Action step: Take one small step each day towards embracing the unknown and facing your fears, knowing that these challenges have the potential to unlock a new level of growth and transformation in your life.

93

Reflection

Look for the wins in everything that happens for you. Sometimes they will be obvious, and sometimes they may be hidden, but somewhere, they are there.

Life can be a rollercoaster of experiences, and it's natural to get caught up in the challenges and setbacks we encounter.

However, by looking for the wins in everything that happens *for* us, we can shift our perspective and focus on the positive aspects of our experiences. Sometimes the wins may be obvious, such as achieving a goal or overcoming a challenge. Other times, they may be more subtle, such as learning a valuable lesson or gaining a new insight.

Regardless of the form they take, the wins are always there if we look for them. By focusing on the wins, we can cultivate a sense of gratitude and appreciation for the many blessings in our lives, and develop a more positive and optimistic outlook.

This can help us to stay motivated and inspired, even in the face of adversity, and to keep moving forward towards our goals and dreams.

In order to look for the wins, it can be helpful to take a step back and reflect on our experiences, asking ourselves what we have learned, what we have gained, and what we are grateful for. By doing so, we can shift our focus from the challenges and setbacks to the many positive aspects of our lives, and cultivate a greater sense of happiness and fulfilment.

Journal prompt: Take a moment to reflect on your recent experiences and identify at least one win or positive aspect in each situation, no matter how small, and express gratitude for it in your journal.

94

Balance II

All transformation/healing/recovery/growth is achieved through a balance of inner and outer work.

Transformation, healing, recovery, and growth are all complex and multifaceted processes that require a balance of both inner and outer work.

The inner work involves looking within ourselves and addressing the emotional, psychological, and spiritual aspects of our being. This may include practices such as meditation, therapy, journaling, or introspection, as well as addressing past traumas and limiting beliefs.

By doing the inner work, we can cultivate greater self-awareness, self-acceptance, and inner peace, which are essential for our overall well-being and personal growth.

The outer work involves taking action and making changes in our external circumstances. This may include developing new habits, changing our environment, or setting boundaries in our relationships.

Both inner and outer work are essential for transformation, healing, recovery, and growth. Without the inner work, we may find ourselves stuck in old patterns and beliefs that limit our potential. Without the outer work, we may struggle to create real-world changes that support our growth and development.

Action step: Take time each day to engage in both inner and outer work, dedicating moments for self-reflection, introspection, and healing practices, as well as taking action towards positive changes in your external circumstances.

95

Silence

Find silence and stillness in your life and you will start to hear your God-self.

In the hustle and bustle of our modern world, it can be easy to get caught up in the noise and chaos of our daily lives.

We are bombarded with endless stimuli, from social media notifications to the constant hum of traffic and the demands of work and family. In the midst of all this noise, it can be hard to connect with our inner selves and our spiritual nature.

However, finding silence and stillness in our lives is essential if we want to connect with our God-self. When we take the time to be still and quiet, we create a space for our inner voice to be heard. This can be achieved through meditation, prayer, or simply taking a few moments to sit in silence and focus on our breath.

In the silence, we can begin to let go of the distractions and noise of the outside world and turn our attention inward. Here, we may find clarity, peace, and a deeper connection with our spiritual nature. We can begin to hear the voice of our intuition, our higher self, and the divine wisdom that lies within us.

By finding silence and stillness in our lives, we can tap into our inner wisdom and connect with our God-self. We can cultivate a deeper sense of peace and purpose, and find guidance and support on our life's journey. So take some time each day to be still and quiet, and allow your inner voice to be heard.

> **Journal Prompt**: Reflect on the importance of finding silence and stillness in your daily life amidst the chaos of the modern world. Consider the distractions and noise that surround you, and how they impact your ability to connect with your inner self and your spiritual nature.

96

Release II

If something or someone is triggering an unwanted emotion within you, do the work to release that emotion and it will be immediately replaced by the unlimited supply of divine love.

We all experience difficult emotions at times, and these emotions can be triggered by a variety of things - from events and situations in our lives to the behaviour of others.

When we experience these emotions, it can be tempting to suppress them or push them aside, but this can lead to long-term negative effects on our mental and emotional well-being.

One powerful approach to dealing with these unwanted

emotions is to do the work to release them. This can involve a variety of techniques, such as mindfulness, journaling, EFT or talking to a trusted friend or therapist. By bringing our attention to these emotions and exploring their root causes, we can begin to release them and find greater peace and clarity.

As we release these unwanted emotions, we create a space for something new and positive to enter our lives. In this case, the unlimited supply of divine love that is always available to us. This love can help us to heal and grow and can bring us greater peace, joy, and fulfilment.

By doing the work to release unwanted emotions, we create a pathway for divine love to enter our lives. This can be a powerful tool for transformation and growth and can help us to live our lives with greater ease and grace.

Action Step: Take proactive steps to release unwanted emotions by engaging in practices such as mindfulness, journaling, EFT (Emotional Freedom Techniques), or seeking support from a trusted friend or therapist, to create space for the influx of divine love, healing, and personal growth in your life.

97

Change

> *If you want to make a change in your life, you have the opportunity at any moment to start. How about starting now?*

Change (aka transformation) is something that many of us seek in our lives.

Whether it's a change in career, a change in our relationships, or a change in our personal habits, it can be easy to put off taking action and fall into a state of complacency. But the truth is that we have the power to make changes at any moment.

If you want to make a change in your life, the best time to

start is always now. The present moment is all that we truly have, and every moment is an opportunity for growth and transformation. By making a change today, you can set yourself on a new path towards a brighter future.

Of course, change can seem to be challenging, and it can be useful to set achievable steps towards your desired outcome. By taking these small incremental steps consistently, you can build momentum and create a sense of progress that can help keep you motivated and inspired; which in turn builds positive energy

So if you're ready to make a change in your life, don't wait for the "perfect" moment or the "right" circumstances. Decide that today, is that moment, decide today that the circumstances are right, and begin to transform your life for the better.

Remember that change is always possible, and that you have the power to make it happen. It starts with a decision.

> **Journal Prompt**: Reflect on a change you desire in your life and explore why you may have been putting it off. Consider the power of the present moment and how starting today can set you on a path towards transformation. Describe the small, achievable steps you can take right now to initiate that change and explore how you can build momentum to keep moving forward.

98

Consciousness

See the potentiality in all moments and all things.
Divine consciousness is everywhere and in all things
in every moment. Relish in the exquisiteness of life.

Life is full of moments, big and small, that can be either overlooked or celebrated.

It's easy to get caught up in the busyness and distractions of daily life and to forget to appreciate the beauty and potentiality of every moment and everything. But the truth is that every moment and everything is infused with divine consciousness, and has the potential to reveal its exquisiteness to us.

By cultivating a mindset of awareness and appreciation, we can learn to see the potentiality in all moments and all things. We can learn to recognise the divine spark that resides within each of us and within everything around us. We can learn to relish in the exquisiteness of life and to approach every moment with a sense of wonder and awe.

This mindset of appreciation can help us to feel more connected to the world around us, and to experience a deeper sense of meaning and purpose in our lives. It can help us to recognise the beauty and potentiality in every person we meet, every task we undertake, and every experience we have.

Take a moment to pause, to breathe, and to appreciate the exquisiteness of life. See the potentiality in all moments and all things, and let the divine consciousness within you guide you towards a more joyful, fulfilling, and meaningful life.

> **Action Prompt**: Pause for a moment, take a deep breath, and consciously appreciate the beauty and potentiality of the present moment, recognising the divine spark within yourself and everything around you, allowing it to guide you towards a more joyful and meaningful life.

99

Consciousness II

> *The relationship within yourself to divine conscious-*
> *ness is a continuous journey, it is never done. Enjoy*
> *the journey in all its glory.*

The relationship within yourself and divine consciousness is a journey that lasts a lifetime.

It's a path that you embark on the moment you become aware of your own existence, and it's a journey that will continue as long as you live. The beauty of this journey is that it's never done, and it's never too late to begin.

At times, the journey may seem easy, with moments of pure joy and connection to the divine. At other times, it may feel like a struggle, with obstacles and challenges that test your faith and commitment. But through it all, it's important to remember that this journey is an opportunity to grow, to learn, and to deepen your understanding of yourself and the universe.

The key to enjoying the journey is to remain present in every moment and to appreciate the beauty of each step along the way. Try your best to cultivate a sense of gratitude and wonder, and to approach each day with an open heart and an open mind. By doing so, you will be able to recognise the divine consciousness within yourself.

Embrace the journey, with all of its ups and downs. Enjoy the beauty and wonder of every moment, and stay committed to your own growth and development. Remember that the relationship within yourself and divine consciousness is a continuous journey and that the journey itself is a gift.

> Journal Prompt: Reflect on your personal journey of discovering and deepening your relationship with divine consciousness. Explore the highs and lows, the moments of joy and struggle, and how they have shaped your understanding of yourself and the universe. Consider the importance of remaining present, cultivating gratitude, and approaching each day with an open heart and mind. Describe the ways in which this ongoing journey has enriched your life and how you can continue to embrace and appreciate its beauty and wonder.

100

Emotional Intelligence II

*Learn the power of advanced emotional intelligence.
It is one of the most empowering, life-changing tools
you will ever possess.*

Emotional intelligence is a vital skill that can positively impact various areas of your life.

This skill involves being able to understand and manage your own emotions, as well as empathise with others on a deeper level and it is rooted in the concept that emotions are energy in motion (e-motion). Through an understanding of this concept, it is possible to develop an advanced emotional intelligence, which can help you to communicate more effectively, build deeper and more meaningful relationships, potentially heal yourself from past traumas, and use your emotions to guide you towards your desires.

An advanced emotional intelligence enables you to become more self-aware and identify and work through any negative patterns or limiting beliefs that may be holding you back. It also helps you maintain emotional balance and flow of energy around the body, allowing you to handle stress and adversity with more ease.

Therefore, recognising the importance of energy in motion and maintaining and interpreting energetic signals is crucial in developing advanced emotional intelligence. By doing so, you can transform your life in profound ways.

Action Step: Cultivate advanced emotional intelligence by practicing self-awareness, identifying and releasing negative patterns or limiting beliefs, and maintaining energetic balance through techniques such as meditation, mindfulness, and energy healing modalities, to positively transform your communication, relationships, and overall well-being.

101

Adventure

Allow adventure to enter your life as it can open up new experiences. Life is for living.

Life is a journey that is meant to be lived to the fullest.

One way to make the most out of life is to allow adventure to enter into your life.

Adventure can take on many forms, whether it is travelling to new places, trying new experiences, or meeting new people.

When you allow adventure to enter into your life, you open yourself up to new experiences and opportunities that you may not have otherwise experienced. You may discover new passions, develop new skills, or meet new people who inspire and challenge you in ways you never thought possible.

It's important to remember that life is short, and we only have a limited time on this earth. By embracing adventure, you can create memories that will last a lifetime and ensure that you are living your life to the fullest.

Of course, stepping outside of your comfort zone and trying new things can be scary, but it's important to take that first step. Once you do, you will find that the rewards of adventure far outweigh any fear or uncertainty.

> Journal Prompt: Reflect on the role of adventure in your life and how it can enhance your journey of living life to the fullest. Explore what adventure means to you, whether it's travelling, trying new experiences, or stepping out of your comfort zone. Describe a specific adventure you would like to embark on and why it excites you. Consider any fears or uncertainties holding you back and how you can overcome them to embrace the rewards and growth that come with adventure.

102

Mindset

Anything is possible with the right mindset, determination, acceptance, surrender and grace. Anyone is capable of anything.

The power of the human mind is truly incredible.

With the right mindset, determination, acceptance, surrender, and grace, anything is possible. This is not just a catchy phrase, but a truth that has been demonstrated time and time again throughout history and certainly a truth that I experienced first-hand as I rebuilt my life after a stroke.

When we cultivate a mindset of positivity and possibility, we begin to see the world in a different light. Rather than focusing on limitations, we start to see opportunities and potential. We recognise that challenges are simply opportunities for growth, and setbacks are not failures, but rather, stepping stones on the path to success.

But having the right mindset alone is not enough. We must also be determined to achieve our goals, accepting of the challenges we face along the way, and willing to surrender our preconceptions and biases. We must approach our pursuits with a sense of grace, understanding that failure is a natural part of the process and that success is not always achieved in a straight line.

With these qualities, anyone is capable of achieving anything they set their mind to. Whether it is pursuing a lifelong dream, overcoming a difficult obstacle, or simply making positive changes in our lives, the power of the human spirit is truly limitless.

> **Action Step**: Cultivate a mindset of positivity and possibility, combined with determination, acceptance of challenges, surrendering preconceptions, and embracing grace, to tap into the incredible power of your mind and unlock limitless potential for achieving your goals and making positive changes in your life.

103

Focus II

> *There may be distractions along the journey of transformation but stick at it and don't ever stop. Keep moving forward and don't give up.*

The journey of transformation can be a long and winding road and full of ups and downs.

There may be times when you face distractions that threaten to take you off course, but it's important to stay committed and keep moving forward. Don't give up on your dreams and aspirations, no matter how difficult the journey may seem.

It's important to remember that setbacks and challenges are a natural part of the transformation process. These obstacles are opportunities for growth and learning, and can even be catalysts for achieving greater success. The key is to maintain a positive attitude, stay focused on your goals, and never lose sight of what you truly want.

When you encounter distractions, take a step back and reassess your priorities. Refocus your energy and attention on what really matters to you, and let go of anything that is holding you back. Keep your eyes on the prize and stay determined to overcome any obstacles that come your way.

Ultimately, the journey of transformation is a rewarding one, filled with personal growth and self-discovery. Embrace the challenges and keep moving forward, and you'll be amazed at how much you can accomplish when you never give up on yourself.

Journal Prompt: Reflect on your personal journey of transformation and growth, acknowledging the ups and downs you have encountered along the way. Consider the distractions and challenges that have threatened to derail your progress, and explore how you have stayed committed and resilient.

104

Brilliance

You have the power of divine consciousness running through you at all times and you are brilliant in your humanness.

As human beings, we often forget the incredible power and potential that resides within us.

We are endowed with the power of divine consciousness, a force that runs through us at all times, guiding and shaping our experiences.

Divine consciousness is the underlying force that governs the universe, the energy that gives rise to all existence. It is the essence of life, and we are privileged to have it within us. This power allows us to tap into our highest potential, to connect with the world around us in a deep and meaningful way.

Despite our many imperfections, we are brilliant in our humanness. We have the capacity for immense creativity, innovation, and growth. We are capable of developing deep relationships with others, of experiencing joy and love, and of making meaningful contributions to the world.

It is essential that we recognise and honour this power within ourselves. By doing so, we can tap into our true potential and live a life that is both fulfilling and purposeful.

We must remember that we are not limited by our circumstances or our past experiences, but rather by our own thoughts and beliefs.

> **Action Step:** Embrace the incredible power within you by cultivating a mindset of limitless potential, letting go of self-limiting thoughts and beliefs, and embracing the brilliance of your humanness. Connect with the divine consciousness that flows through you, allowing it to guide and shape your experiences. Believe in your capacity for growth, creativity, and meaningful connections, and take inspired action towards living a fulfilling and purposeful life.

105

Stretch

The practice of yoga has been known to have transformative effects on the mind and body.

The practice of yoga is an ancient discipline that has been recognised for its transformative effects on the mind and body. Yoga combines physical postures, breath control, and meditation to enhance overall well-being.

Yoga practice promotes physical health by improving flexibility, strength, and balance. Regular practice can also reduce stress, anxiety, and depression, leading to a calmer and more centred state of mind.

In addition to physical benefits, yoga also promotes mental

and emotional well-being. Yoga practice cultivates mindfulness, which can help increase self-awareness, emotional regulation, and overall mental clarity.

Furthermore, the practice of yoga has been shown to have transformative effects on individuals who struggle with addiction, trauma, and chronic pain. It can help individuals cope with difficult emotions and manage stress in a healthy and constructive way.

Overall, the practice of yoga has transformative effects on the mind and body. It promotes physical, mental, and emotional well-being, and can help individuals cope with challenges in their lives. By incorporating yoga practice into daily routines, individuals can enjoy the transformative benefits that this ancient discipline has to offer.

> **Journal Prompt:** Reflect on your experience with yoga and how it has transformed your mind and body. Consider the physical improvements you have noticed, such as increased flexibility and strength, as well as the mental and emotional changes, such as reduced stress and enhanced self-awareness. Explore how incorporating yoga into your daily routine has positively impacted your overall well-being and transformed your perspective on life.

106

Worthiness II

Don't ever look at something as being not good enough. Everything has value and worth.

It is easy to fall into the trap of viewing things as not good enough, especially in a society that values perfection and success.

However, it is important to recognise that everything has value and worth, no matter how small or seemingly insignificant. When we view something as not good enough, we are placing a judgment on it based on our own expectations and standards. This can lead to feelings of disappointment and frustration and can prevent us from seeing the true value of the thing in question.

Remember that everything has its own unique qualities and characteristics that make it valuable and worthwhile. Even the smallest things can have a profound impact on our lives and bring us joy and happiness.

When we learn to appreciate the value and worth of all things, we open ourselves up to new opportunities and experiences. We become more open-minded and accepting, and are able to see the beauty and potential in everything around us.

It is important to shift our mindset from viewing things as not good enough to recognising the inherent value and worth in all things. By doing so, we can cultivate a greater sense of gratitude, joy, and fulfilment in our lives, and appreciate the beauty and potential in everything around us.

Action Step: Practice shifting your mindset from judgment to appreciation by consciously seeking and acknowledging the value and worth in all things, big or small, and embracing gratitude for the beauty and potential they bring to your life.

107

Support III

It's okay to admit that you need help. Trying to push on when it feels wrong or stressful can do more harm than good. Go easy on yourself and let others help.

In our culture, there can be a tendency to view asking for help as a sign of weakness or failure.

However, it is important to recognise that we all need help at times and that trying to push on when we are struggling can do more harm than good.

When we refuse to ask for help, we are denying ourselves

the support and resources that we need to overcome our challenges.

This can lead to feelings of overwhelm, stress, and burn-out, which can have serious consequences on all aspects of well-being.

It is important to go easy on ourselves and recognise that it is okay to ask for help. Whether it is seeking support from friends and family, or seeking professional help from a coach, mentor, therapist or counsellor, there are many resources available to us when we need them.

When we allow ourselves to ask for help, we open ourselves up to new opportunities for growth and healing. We become more resilient, adaptable, and able to navigate the challenges of life with greater ease and grace.

By doing so, we can cultivate a greater sense of self-awareness and self-compassion, and live a more fulfilling and meaning-ful life.

Journal Prompt: Reflect on your beliefs and attitudes about asking for help. Explore any resistance or fears you may have, and consider the benefits and oppor-tunities that can arise when you embrace the idea of seeking support and reaching out for help in times of need.

108

Becoming II

> *Live as if the transformation has already happened
> and then it happens.*

The idea of living as if the transformation has already happened is a powerful one.

It is a mindset that can help us to shift our perspective, overcome our fears, and achieve our goals.

When we live as if the transformation has already happened, we are embodying the qualities and characteristics of the person we want to become. We are visualising ourselves as successful, happy, and fulfilled, and acting in a way that aligns with that vision.

By doing this, we are setting in motion the forces of the universe to help us achieve our goals. We are opening ourselves up to new opportunities and experiences that can help us to become the person we want to be.

Living as if the transformation has already happened can also help us to overcome our fears and doubts. It can give us the courage and confidence to take risks and pursue our dreams, even when the path ahead is uncertain.

Action Step: Take a moment to visualise and embody the person you want to become. Act as if the transformation has already occurred, and make choices and decisions that align with that vision. Embrace courage and embrace the unknown, knowing that you are moving closer to your desired transformation.

109

Celebrate II

Capture the moment and the memories so that you can celebrate your progress time and time again.

In our fast-paced and constantly changing world, it is easy to lose sight of our progress and the moments that matter most.

However, by capturing the moment and the memories, we can celebrate our progress time and time again.

When we take the time to capture the moment, we are creating a tangible reminder of our progress and the experiences that have shaped us. Whether it is through journaling, a diary, taking photographs, or creating art, capturing the moment allows us to look back on our journey with clarity and appreciation.

Capturing any moment can help with celebrating our progress. By celebrating we are creating a positive feedback loop that can fuel our motivation and inspiration. We emit a positive signal to which even greater positivity will be attracted.

When we see how far we have come and the challenges we have overcome, we are more likely to continue moving forward and pursuing our goals.

Capturing the memories can also be a powerful tool for personal growth and self-reflection. By looking back on our experiences and the lessons we have learned, we can gain new insights and perspectives that can help us to grow and evolve as individuals.

> **Action Step**: Take a moment today to capture a meaningful moment or memory through journaling, photography, or any creative medium that resonates with you, and reflect on your progress and the lessons learned. Celebrate the journey and use it as motivation to continue moving forward.

Rest

There are times when you can and should give yourself a break. Take the break and seize the moment for you deserve it.

In our hectic and high-pressure society, it is easy to feel overwhelmed and burnt out. Therefore, it is important to recognise that there are times when you can and should give yourself a break.

Taking the time to rest and recharge can help you to regain your energy and focus, and enable you to continue moving forward in a more productive and fulfilling way.

When you give yourself a break, you are acknowledging the

importance of self-care and taking care of your own well-being. It is not a sign of weakness or failure, but rather a necessary step in maintaining your physical, mental, and emotional health.

Seizing the moment to take a break can also help you cultivate a greater sense of self-awareness and self-compassion. By recognising your own limits and needs, you are developing a deeper understanding of yourself and your own unique journey.

So go ahead, take the break you deserve and give yourself the gift of rest and rejuvenation.

> **Journal Prompt:** Reflect on a time when you felt overwhelmed or burnt out, and explore ways in which you can give yourself a break and prioritise self-care to regain your energy and maintain your well-being. How can you incorporate rest and rejuvenation into your daily life to cultivate a healthier balance?

111

Manifestation

If you want to manifest a new reality, start with the idea. Fuel the idea with intention and energy and then take the aligned action to realise that reality.

The power of manifestation is a fairly well-known concept. The basic principle behind manifestation is that we have the ability to create our own reality by focusing our thoughts, intentions, and energy on a desired outcome.

To manifest a new reality, we must start with the idea. We must have a clear vision of what we want to create and focus our thoughts and intentions on that vision. We must also infuse that idea with positive energy and emotions, such as gratitude, joy, and love, to create a powerful energetic charge.

However, manifestation is not just about positive thinking and visualisation. We must also take aligned action to make our vision a reality. This means taking the necessary steps, making the right decisions, and being open to new opportunities and experiences that can help us achieve our desired outcome.

The key to successful manifestation is finding the balance between intention, infused energy (emotions) and action. We must have a clear idea of what we want, we must feel the emotion of being in or having the idea in reality, and then further ideas and inspiration will come to us from which to take the "inspired" action(s).

Remember, the power to manifest your dreams lies within you. As creative human beings, we are manifesting our reality in every moment, so the secret is awareness of your predominant thoughts, feelings and actions.

> **Action step**: Take a moment to reflect on your desires and aspirations, and identify one small, actionable step you can take today to align your thoughts, intentions, and actions towards manifesting your desired outcome.

112

Present II

> *Nothing is forever. Everything is transient. Make the most of every moment.*

Life is a constantly changing and evolving journey. Everything around us, from our relationships to our surroundings, is in a state of constant flux.

The truth is that nothing is forever, and everything is transient. However, this does not mean that we should feel disheartened or disillusioned. Instead, it is a reminder to make the most of every moment.

The impermanence of life is what makes it precious and valuable. It is what gives our experiences and relationships their depth and richness. It is also what reminds us of the importance of being present and mindful in every moment.

By embracing the transient nature of life, we can learn to appreciate the little moments, find joy in the ordinary, and cherish the people and experiences that make our lives meaningful. We can learn to let go of attachments and expectations and instead focus on living fully in the present moment.

By embracing the impermanence of life, we can find a deeper sense of appreciation and gratitude for the people and experiences that make our lives meaningful. We can learn to let go of attachments and expectations and focus on being fully present in every moment. Remember, the only moment that truly exists is the present moment, so make the most of it while it lasts.

> **Journal prompt**: Reflect on the transient nature of life and consider how you can embrace the present moment, find joy in the ordinary, and cultivate a deeper sense of appreciation and gratitude for the people and experiences that make your life meaningful.

113

Growth

> *Develop the techniques that will serve you for life.*
> *They can save your life, transform your life and they*
> *are tools that will serve you and your loved ones for-*
> *ever.*

In life, we face many challenges and obstacles that require us to develop specific techniques and skills to overcome them.

Whether it's learning how to manage stress, build resilience, or communicate effectively, these techniques can serve us for life.

Developing techniques that serve us for life means investing time and energy in learning and practicing new skills. It means being open to trying new things, taking risks, and being willing to make mistakes and learn from them.

The benefits of developing techniques that serve us for life are numerous. They can help us manage difficult emotions, cope with challenging situations, and build healthier relationships. They can also give us a sense of purpose, fulfilment, and self-confidence.

Moreover, the techniques that we develop can be passed down to our loved ones, making them tools that serve not only ourselves but those around us as well. By modelling and sharing our knowledge and skills, we can create a positive ripple effect that impacts the lives of others and makes the world a better place.

> **Action step**: Take proactive steps to develop techniques and skills that serve you for life, such as investing time in learning, practicing new skills, and being open to trying new things, so that you can effectively overcome challenges, manage stress, and build resilience.

114

Stillness

Only when we still our minds can we allow our God-self voice to filter through.

Our minds are constantly in a state of flux, processing information, making decisions, and responding to stimuli.

However, in the midst of this constant activity, it can be challenging to connect with our inner voice, that part of ourselves that is connected to something greater than ourselves.

The key to accessing this inner voice is by stilling our minds. By quieting the constant chatter and noise of our thoughts, we create space for our God-self to filter through. This is where we can connect with our intuition, our inner wisdom, and our deepest values and beliefs.

When we still our minds, we allow ourselves to be fully present in the moment. We can let go of worries and distractions and focus on what is truly important. This can help us gain clarity and perspective, and make better decisions in our lives.

Moreover, stilling our minds can have a profound impact on our spiritual and emotional well-being. It can help us connect with something greater than ourselves, and foster a sense of inner peace and calmness.

This can help us navigate life's challenges with greater resilience and grace.

> **Journal prompt:** Reflect on the importance of stilling your mind and connecting with your inner voice. How can you incorporate moments of stillness into your daily life to cultivate inner peace, clarity, and a deeper connection with yourself and something greater than yourself?

115

Courage II

> *When you stand up and face your fears, your fears then melt away right before your eyes; it was all make-believe in your mind. In that salvation can lie the source of true happiness.*

Fears and anxieties can be powerful forces in our lives, often preventing us from taking risks, pursuing our dreams, and experiencing true happiness.

However, when we stand up and face our fears, something magical happens - they often melt away right before our eyes.

This is because our fears are often based on imagined scenarios and worst-case outcomes that rarely come to fruition. By facing our fears head-on, we can break the cycle of anxiety and see that our fears are simply illusions.

In that salvation can lie the source of true happiness. By confronting our fears and realising that they were only illusions, we can free ourselves from the grip of anxiety and move forward with confidence and courage.

This can lead to a sense of liberation and empowerment that can enhance every aspect of our lives.

Moreover, facing our fears can help us grow and develop as individuals. By overcoming obstacles and challenges, we gain a sense of self-mastery and resilience, which can lead to a greater sense of purpose and fulfilment.

Action step: Take a moment to identify one fear or anxiety that is holding you back, and commit to facing it head-on. Take a small step today towards confronting that fear, and witness the transformative power it has in your life.

116

Love VI

Expand the universe with your loving energy and your life will become enriched with love and goodness.

The universe is a vast and mysterious place, full of wonder and beauty. As we navigate our way through life, we have the power to expand the universe with our loving energy, and in doing so, we can enrich our lives with love and goodness.

Love is a powerful force that can transform lives and inspire positive change. When we approach the world with a loving and compassionate heart, we create a ripple effect that can touch the lives of countless others. Our loving energy can inspire others to be kind, compassionate, and caring, and in doing so, we can create a more loving and peaceful world.

Moreover, when we expand the universe with our loving energy, we create a sense of interconnectedness with all that is around us. We begin to see the world through a lens of love and goodness, and in doing so, we attract more love and goodness into our lives.

Expanding the universe with our loving energy requires a conscious effort to approach the world with an open heart and a desire to make a positive difference. It requires us to let go of fear, judgment, and negativity, and to embrace the power of love to transform our lives and the world around us.

> Journal prompt: Reflect on a moment when you shared your loving energy with others and experienced its transformative power. How did it enrich your life and create a positive impact on the world around you?

117

Empowerment II

You do you, and let me do me. Don't ever feel pressured to do anything you don't REALLY want to do. You have your own mind to make your own decisions.

In a world where we are bombarded with endless expectations, it can be easy to lose sight of our own wants and needs.

However, it is essential to remember that our lives are our own, and we have the power to make our own decisions.

It is okay to say no to things that we do not want to do, even if others may not understand. Our personal growth and happiness should be a priority, and we should not feel pressured to do things that do not align with our values or goals.

We should trust our instincts and be true to ourselves. Our individuality and unique perspectives are what make us valuable to the world. Embracing our true selves and making our own choices can lead to a more fulfilling and purposeful life.

We should remember that our decisions have consequences, both positive and negative. It is important to take responsibility for the choices we make and understand that they shape our lives. Making our own decisions empowers us and helps us take control of our lives.

Action step: Take a moment to reflect on your own wants and needs, and identify one thing you can say no to that does not align with your values or goals. Practice asserting your boundaries and making decisions that prioritise your personal growth and happiness.

118

Attitude

▌ *Develop an unshakeable positive attitude towards life, which will pay you huge dividends.* ▌

Developing an unshakeable positive attitude towards life can be a game-changer. It can influence the way we think, feel, and behave, and ultimately lead to a more fulfilling life.

A positive attitude allows us to approach challenges and setbacks with optimism and resilience. It helps us see opportunities where others see roadblocks and can help us persevere through tough times.

With a positive attitude, we can shift our focus towards solutions and possibilities, instead of dwelling on problems.

Moreover, a positive attitude can also have a profound impact on our relationships. It can attract positive people and experiences, and make us more likeable and approachable. It can also improve our communication and problem-solving skills and make us more effective at work and in our personal lives.

The benefits of a positive attitude extend beyond our personal and professional lives. It can also improve our physical health, reduce stress and anxiety, and boost our immune system.

By cultivating positivity and optimism, we can approach life with a sense of excitement and purpose, leading to a more fulfilling and rewarding life.

> Journal prompt: Reflect on a recent challenge or setback you have faced, and explore how adopting a positive attitude could have influenced your perspective and outcomes. Consider how cultivating a positive attitude can impact various areas of your life and bring about positive changes.

119

Growth II

Nothing happens to you, it all happens for you at some level. Taking this view will give you the spiritual fuel to recover, heal, learn and grow.

Adopting the belief that nothing happens to us, but rather, everything happens for us, can have a profound impact on our outlook on life. It can help us view challenges and difficult experiences as opportunities for growth and transformation, rather than setbacks or obstacles.

When we see life through this lens, we understand that every experience, good or bad, has a purpose and a lesson for us. Even in the darkest moments of our lives, there is an opportunity for growth and learning. By accepting this, we can use our challenges to fuel our spiritual growth and personal development.

Moreover, this perspective can help us cultivate gratitude and a sense of appreciation for our experiences. Instead of dwelling on the negative, we can focus on the positive lessons and growth that come from every situation. This can help us stay motivated and hopeful, even during difficult times.

By embracing the idea that everything happens for us, we can find meaning and purpose in our experiences. We can learn to trust the universe and have faith that everything is happening for our highest good. Ultimately, this perspective can help us recover, heal, learn and grow, and find greater joy and fulfilment in life.

> **Action step**: Embrace the belief that everything happens for you, and challenge yourself to find the lesson or opportunity for growth in a recent challenging experience you've had.

120

Kindness II

*Let your inner voice of love and kindness dominate
your existence then you will find more evidence to
support that loving worldview.*

Our inner voice is a powerful force in our lives. It can either
support and encourage us, or it can hold us back and create
negative thought patterns.

By choosing to let our inner voice of love and kindness
dominate our existence, we open ourselves up to a world of
positivity, joy, and abundance.

When we operate from a place of love and kindness, we begin
to see the world in a different light. We notice the beauty

and goodness that exists all around us, and we become more attuned to the needs and feelings of others.

This helps us to cultivate deeper relationships, more fulfilling experiences, and a greater sense of purpose. Moreover, when we approach life from a place of love and kindness, we are more likely to attract positive people and experiences into our lives.

Our thoughts and beliefs create our reality, so by focusing on love and kindness, we begin to create a reality that reflects those values.

When we let our inner voice of love and kindness dominate our existence, we tap into a deep well of strength and resilience. We are able to overcome challenges with grace and compassion, and we are better equipped to navigate the ups and downs of life.

> **Journal prompt:** Reflect on a recent situation where you listened to your inner voice of love and kindness, and explore how it influenced your experience and interactions.

121

Trust

Trust in the process. There will be times when you cannot see the results of your efforts, but through trust, persistence and faith you will get there.

Trusting in the process is a crucial part of achieving success in any area of life. There will be times when we put in a lot of effort, yet we don't see immediate results.

It can be discouraging, and it's tempting to give up. However, it's important to remember that success is rarely achieved overnight. Rather, it is the result of persistent effort and faith in the process.

Trusting in the process means staying committed to your

goals, even when progress is slow. It means having faith in your abilities, and in the belief that success is possible. It also means being patient, and accepting that sometimes results take time to manifest.

When we trust in the process, we open ourselves up to new opportunities and experiences. We become more resilient and adaptable, and we are better equipped to handle challenges and setbacks. We also become more attuned to our own intuition and instincts, and we are better able to make wise decisions and take action in alignment with our goals.

So, trust in the process. Have faith in your abilities, and stay committed to your goals, even when progress is slow. Through persistence, faith, and trust, you will get there.

> **Action step**: Take a moment to reflect on an area of your life where you may be feeling impatient or discouraged in your progress. Write down three reasons why you should trust in the process and continue moving forward towards your goals.

122

Miracle II

> *You are the most amazing creature and you are gifted with an incredible brain. Don't ever take that gift for granted.*

As humans, we are incredibly unique and amazing creatures. Our bodies can perform incredible feats, and our brains are the most powerful tool we possess.

The human brain is an incredible gift that allows us to think, create, imagine, and problem-solve. It allows us to experience the world in a way that is both complex and beautiful.

We often go through life without fully appreciating the incredible power and potential of our brains. We get caught up in the day-to-day struggles of life, and we forget just how remarkable we really are.

It's essential to take a step back and reflect on the amazing gift that is our brain. We should remind ourselves of the incredible capabilities we possess and the unlimited potential that lies within us. We should challenge ourselves to continually learn, grow, and expand our brains, and to use our gifts to make a positive impact on the world.

As someone, who has experienced a severe brain injury through stroke, I became acutely aware of both the incredible power of the brain and equally, the (sometimes) awful effects of injury and recovery.

Appreciate your brain, nurture it, and use it to its fullest potential. You are an amazing creature, and you have the power to achieve incredible things.

> Journal prompt: Reflect on three amazing abilities or capabilities of your brain that you are grateful for. How can you nurture and harness these abilities to make a positive impact on your life and the world around you?

123

Trust II

> *Trust that God will provide for you in ways far greater than you can ever imagine.*

Trusting that God will provide for us is an act of faith that can bring great peace and comfort to our lives.

It can be difficult to let go of control and place our trust in something beyond ourselves, but doing so can lead to a greater sense of purpose and security.

Believing that divine intelligence will provide for us in ways far greater than we can imagine means having faith that beyond any hardship there is a great gift in the form of wisdom and a greater knowing. It means trusting that the challenges we face are part of a greater purpose and that there is always a way forward, even when we cannot see it.

When we trust in a provision from a higher source, we can approach life with a greater sense of peace and gratitude. We can focus on the present moment and be open to the opportunities and blessings that come our way. We can let go of our fears and worries and have faith that we will be taken care of, no matter what.

But that doesn't mean we can relinquish any responsibility. We must work together with divine intelligence to create a reality that we desire. Additionally, trusting in God's provision does not mean that we will never face difficulties or challenges, but it does mean that we can face them with a greater sense of hope and resilience.

Action step: Take a moment to surrender control and place your trust in a higher power. Reflect on one specific area of your life where you can let go of worry and fear and choose to have faith that divine provision will guide and support you. Take a step forward with a renewed sense of peace and trust.

124

Celebrate III

People will be shocked at your transformation and many will want to celebrate you.

Transformation is a powerful process that can change a person's life in unimaginable ways. When you decide to embark on a journey of self-discovery and transformation, you will likely encounter numerous challenges that will test your resolve.

However, if you persist through these obstacles, you will emerge on the other side as a new and improved version of yourself.

The beauty of transformation is that it is often evident to

others. When people see the positive changes you have made, they will be surprised and inspired by your transformation. They will see how far you have come and be amazed at the person you have become.

Moreover, your transformation will not only inspire others, but it will also give them hope that they too can change their lives for the better. People may come to you seeking advice on how to transform their own lives, and you can use your experience to help guide and motivate them.

Your transformation will not only be a personal accomplishment but also a gift to the people around you.

So, trust in the process and keep moving forward with determination and purpose. Your journey may surprise you, and others, in the most wonderful ways.

> **Journal prompt:** Reflect on a transformative experience in your life and the challenges you faced along the way. How did you grow and evolve as a person? Consider the impact of your transformation on yourself and those around you, and how it has inspired others.

This Transformation Key Subject Index is designed to help you navigate to any specific transformation key based on its subject.

For example, if you want to focus on being more present in your life then look up the transformation keys under the subject of "Present", or if you want to generate a greater sense of worthiness then look up the transformation keys under the subject of "Worthiness". Perhaps you are noticing that you are becoming more aware of your emotions, in that case, you might want to refer to the transformation keys associated with "Emotional Intelligence" and "Emotions".

Please use this subject index as you navigate different aspects and phases of your life and personal transformation.

THE TRANSFORMATION KEY SUBJECT INDEX